ALIENS *in the*
PROMISED LAND

Nathan,

You are a true friend!! Thanks so much for coming out tonight!! Your support is greatly appreciated!. Blessings on you + your family!!

5/14/2013

ALSO BY ANTHONY B. BRADLEY

Liberating Black Theology (2010)

Black and Tired (2011)

Keep Your Head Up (2012)

The Political Economy of Liberation (2012)

ALIENS *in the* PROMISED LAND

Why Minority Leadership
Is Overlooked *in* White Christian
Churches *and* Institutions

EDITED BY
ANTHONY B. BRADLEY

PUBLISHING
P.O. BOX 817 • PHILLIPSBURG • NEW JERSEY 08865-0817

ISBN: 978-1-59638-234-3 (pbk)
ISBN: 978-1-59638-623-5 (ePub)
ISBN: 978-1-59638-624-2 (Mobi)

"Precious Puritans" is quoted with permission from the artist, Jason Petty (Propaganda), and from Humble Beast Records.

The material of the appendix, "Racism and the Church," is used with permission from the secretary of The Lutheran Church–Missouri Synod.

Cover images: arch © Ingram Publishing / Jupiterimages; paper © istockphoto.com / David Schrader

Text images: holy Bible image © istockphoto.com / Dawn Hudson; shrugging man image © istockphoto.com / Brett Lamb

Printed in the United States of America

Library of Congress Cataloging-in-Publication Data

Bradley, Anthony B., 1971-
  Aliens in the promised land : why minority leadership is overlooked in white Christian churches and institutions / edited by Anthony B. Bradley.
     pages cm
  Includes bibliographical references and index.
  ISBN 978-1-59638-234-3 (pbk.)
  1. Christian leadership. 2. Church and minorities. 3. Diversity in the workplace. I. Title.
  BV652.1.B734 2013
  262'.1089--dc23
                        2013008150

To New City Fellowship,
Chattanooga, Tennessee

Precious Puritans

If you would allow me a second to deal with some in-
house issues,
Pastor, it's hard for me when you quote Puritans.
Oh the precious Puritans!
Have you not noticed our facial expressions?
One of bewilderment and heartbreak.
Not you too, pastor.

You know they were the chaplains on slave ships.
Would you quote Columbus to Cherokees?
Would you quote Cortez to Aztecs?
Even if his theology was good?
It just sings of your blind privilege, would you agree?
Your precious Puritans.

They looked my onyx and bronze-skinned forefathers
in their face—
Their polytheistic, God-hating face,
Shackled, diseased, imprisoned face—
And taught a gospel that says God had multiple images
in mind when he created us in it.
Their fore-destined salvation contains a contentment in
the stage they were given, which is to be owned by your
forefathers' superior, image-bearing face,
Says your precious Puritans.

And my anger towards this teaching screams of an
immature doctrine and a misunderstanding of the
gospel. I should be content, right? Isn't that what
Paul taught?
According to your precious Puritans.

You get it, but you don't get it.
Oh that we can go back to the America we once were,
 founded on Christian values.
They don't build preachers like we used to. The richness
 of their revelation.
It must be nice to not have to think or consider race.
It must have been nice to have the time to contemplate
 the stars.

Pastor, your colorless rhetoric is a cop-out.
You see my skin, and I see yours and they are beautiful,
Fearfully and wonderfully, divinely designed uniqueness.
Shouldn't we celebrate it rather than act like it ain't there?
I get it. Your Puritans got it. But . . .

How come the things the Holy Spirit showed them in
 the valley of vision didn't compel them to knock in
 they neighbors' door and tell them they can't own
 people?
Your precious Puritans were not perfect.
You romanticize them like they were inerrant. As if the
 skeletons in their closet is pardoned due to their hard
 work and tobacco growth.
As if the abolitionists weren't racist and just pro union.
As if God only spoke to white boys with epic beards!
You know Jesus didn't REALLY look like the paintings.
 That was just Michelangelo's boyfriend.
Your precious Puritans.

They got it, but they didn't get it.
There's no one generation of believers that figured out
 the marriage of proper doctrine and action.

Don't pedestal these people. Your precious Puritans'
   partners purchased persons.
Why would you quote them?
Step away. Think of the congregation that quotes you.
   Are you inerrant?
Trust me, I know the feeling.
Same feeling I get when people quote me.
If you only knew!
I get it. But I don't get it.
Ask my wife.

It bothers me when you quote Puritans, honestly, for
   the same reason it bothers me when people quote
   me.
Their precious Propaganda.
I guess God does use crooked sticks to make straight lines.
Just like your precious Puritans.

—Propaganda, from the album
Excellent (Humble Beast Records)

Contents

Acknowledgments

THE IDEA FOR THIS BOOK emerged from various conversations with people from all over America through social media platforms. I would like to thank all my students, friends, and colleagues at The King's College for their support and patience with my being distracted during the production of this book over the past two years. I would particularly like to thank my former student (turned editor), Stephen Wesley, for his superb skill and professionalism in editing this book. My teaching assistants, Joshua Craddock and Christopher Svendsen, deserve special recognition for taking on some additional grading duties while I worked on this project during the year. My friends at Fordham University's Ethics and Society program have been instrumental in giving me new categories for analysis beyond my own tribe of Protestant evangelicals. The past two years of research and study at Fordham have been invaluable for helping me rethink the direction of this project. Finally, I would like to thank Marvin Padgett and my friends at P&R Publishing for taking the risk of publishing a book spanning multiple tribes. It has been great to work with the P&R team!

I

GENERAL INTRODUCTION: MY STORY

Anthony B. Bradley

THIS BOOK EMERGES out of much pain, many wounds, sobered expectations, and yet hope for the future. After my spiritual awakening in college, I had great hopes of serving the church in Christ in the spreading of the gospel. As someone who was young and naive, and who continues to be in many ways (though not so young), I thought—with my own inflated view of my importance to the kingdom—I was going to be able to "make a difference" in helping to diversify Reformed and classical Presbyterian networks.

But I had a sobering wake-up call in 2004, when I received word that John Calvin–loving racists were beginning to post things about me on the Internet. It continues to this day, but the worst of it emerged in 2006. I learned that some of those for whom the Puritans are precious did not welcome my presence among them. On November 27, 2006, the following was posted on a blog about

me: "Afro-Knee Bradley, the PCA darling, is an illiterate nigger."
For several years, while teaching at a Presbyterian seminary in
the Midwest, I repeatedly received racial slurs on the Internet
and on radio programs from many who aligned themselves with
historic Southern Presbyterianism and Calvinism. While I was
aware that racism had been a part of Southern Presbyterian history and Calvinism in general, I had no idea that it remained
alive and well and unchecked in some Reformed and Presbyterian
churches. I was even more surprised to discover that few people
were even talking about it.[1] I began to ask new questions about
the presence of racism in evangelicalism at large, especially among
those who openly boast about the soundness of their theology.
This book represents my ongoing struggle to make sense of why
evangelicalism struggles with diversity in church leadership and
in the Christian academy. To lead this discussion, I have gathered
Hispanic, black, and Asian scholars to describe their own experience as minorities and leaders in evangelical circles and to suggest
ways to make real progress toward racial diversity.

The diversity in the book will be a challenge to some. I am
fully aware that evangelicalism is now tribal, and many of us
value the perspective of leaders from only our particular tribe—
i.e., denomination, theological community, writers from a particular publisher, graduates of certain seminaries, and the like.
The contributors to this book represent multiple tribes in terms
of race and also in terms of church background, ranging from
Baptist to Mennonite to Presbyterian. The representation of
many tribes is a unique feature of this book on Protestant evangelicalism. The challenge for readers will be to read the stories
and understand the hopes from those outside their respective
tribes. I would argue that this is the beauty of the kingdom: that
we have the opportunity to learn from other believers for whom
Christ died and who might not share our denominational space
or network affiliation. This book represents a great opportunity

to learn, especially for those of us who have spent many years in Reformed and Presbyterian associations.

I believe this conversation to be important because, to my surprise, I have encountered resistance even to the idea that the Reformed tradition has ever had any racism in any of its church leaders. It is important to know Christian history, so that we can learn from the past, and so that we don't repeat the same mistakes. We need to know our blind spots and weaknesses. We need to know how those who went before us needed the gospel, so that we might lean on the grace of God and be faithful to what he intends his people to do in our time as well. The Puritans are not precious to all of us. Honesty, confession, and repentance are the way forward. We need to be proactive.

Back when I had an active personal blog,[2] I questioned the silence about racism in broadly Reformed and conservative Presbyterian circles, then in response to my being called a "token negro" (again) on a popular racist website. I received this in an email from a well-known pastor in Reformed circles:

> In the few sentences you wrote you are making Reformed Christians complicit in your charge of racism, and that's a serious thing. If you want to say that Reformed people are racist, you'll need to do better than pointing to one site whose whole *modus operandi* is racism. . . .
>
> I've been Reformed just about all my life [and] I've never seen any hint of racism. Quite the opposite, in fact. I've found this movement systematically combating racism and seeking to be as integrated, as cross-racial and cross-cultural as possible. I could provide a heap of evidence to prove that. I can look to my own church and see a lot of races present and enjoying sweet fellowship together.

What was so surprising to me in the email was the simultaneous confidence in, and ignorance of, his own tradition, given that he has been Reformed nearly his entire life. How can someone be so steeped in the Reformed tradition and never be introduced to how the Reformed tradition's racism gave birth to apartheid in South Africa, how it litters the anthropology of Abraham Kuyper, and how it is explicitly described in the work of R. L. Dabney?[3] It is the cultural and historical ignorance represented by statements like the one above that demonstrates the need for an honest, historically informed conversation. Many white evangelicals are resistant to the fact that racism remains in contexts driven by "the gospel." However, because sin still exists, there is no reason to believe that racism will simply magically disappear or that we simply need to "get over it" and "move on." In evangelicalism, there is a strange tendency to confess that we struggle with other sins, like materialism, anger, gossip, adultery, individualism, and the like, and to rebuke American society because of abortion, homosexuality, alcohol abuse, and so on, yet to ignore the racial issues in our own midst. This book is an attempt to humbly bring an issue that is important to minorities who are within and adjacent to evangelicalism to the attention of those committed to pressing the claims of Christ everywhere in life. This volume is a collection of stories and recommendations from Asian, black, and Hispanic leaders from multiple denominations, who write to help evangelicalism be a more faithful witness to the world in showing that the gospel brings people together in Christ from all tribes, languages, and cultures for a common purpose: to glorify God and enjoy him forever.

Evangelicalism will not make progress unless we listen to the stories and recommendations of ethnic leaders. The Reformed and Presbyterian tradition provides a good example of why this book is needed. Presbyterian denominations in America that subscribe to the Westminster Confession of Faith continue to struggle to diversify because of its cultural captivity, as some might suggest. What is worse, some Reformed and Presbyterian churches not only are culturally captive to white Western norms, but also have embraced the doctrine of the spirituality of the church, which has provided an excuse for not speaking to issues like racial segregation after World War II. Joel Alvis highlights this history in *Religion and Race: Southern Presbyterians, 1946–1983*, as does Peter Slade in *Open Friendship in a Closed Society: Mission, Mississippi, and a Theology of Friendship.*[4] I inadvertently created a denominational firestorm by summarizing Slade's findings on my blog. I was struggling to figure out why someone outside my own denomination knew parts of its history that I had never heard. Slade reports the following:

- Some Presbyterians in Jackson, Mississippi, seem to have played a role in resisting desegregation in Mississippi by embracing the "spirituality of the church" doctrine.[5]

- Rev. James Henry Thornwell issued a call to "reform" slavery, not abolish it.[6]

- On December 4, 1861, the representatives of forty-seven Southern presbyteries formed an Assembly of the Presbyterian Church in the Confederate States of America (PCCSA).[7]

- Mississippi Presbyterians exhibited paternalism toward blacks in the formation of institutions and programs designed to help them.[8]

- First Presbyterian Church in Jackson issued a statement in 1954 rejecting the Presbyterian Church in the United States' support of the conclusion of *Brown v. Board*.[9]

- Dr. Guy T. Gillespie (a former president at Belhaven College) argued in favor of segregation.[10]

- Desegregation led to the launching of Christian schools in Jackson; Mississippi Presbyterians equated supporting desegregation with being a liberal in the 1960s.[11]

The above list does not represent the full story. The story of Presbyterianism in Jackson, Mississippi, should continue to be clarified, and there is good evidence that the future looks bright for discussing race in those circles in the future. Like the Lutheran Church—Missouri Synod in 1994 and the Southern Baptist Convention in 1995, the Presbyterian Church in America passed an overture in 2002 strongly opposing racism and confessing general racism in the past, in an effort to move toward the gospel call to racial reconciliation.[12] The Missouri Synod successfully produced denominational leaders like Dr. John Nunes, the president of Lutheran World Relief. In 2012, the Southern Baptist Convention elected the Rev. Fred Luther as its first black denominational president. Some denominations are making real progress in terms of their leadership in taking action in accordance with their repentance.

The most courageous and unprecedented confession of racism to date in a conservative Presbyterian congregation occurred under the leadership of the Rev. Richie Sessions, senior pastor of Independent Presbyterian Church in Memphis, Tennessee.[13] Independent Presbyterian was founded in early 1965 after the session of Second Presbyterian Church in Memphis reluctantly admitted black worshippers, after it voted to limit the power of elders who were racial hard-liners. These men and their families responded by departing to found Independent Presbyterian, adopting a segregation policy based on the conviction that "the scriptures teach that the separation of nations, peoples and groups will preserve the peace, purity and unity of the Church."[14] After years of leading his church in honesty, confession, and repentance, on Sunday, May 13, 2012, Ruling Elder Sam Graham read this statement:

> On behalf of the Session, this public address to you today specifically marks the beginning of a time of corporate confession and repentance by Independent Presbyterian Church (past and

present) regarding the sin of racism. Just as we celebrate those aspects of our history at Independent Presbyterian Church of which we the Church are proud, we must also acknowledge with sadness and renounce and repudiate those practices in our history that do not reflect biblical standards. We profess, acknowledge and confess before God, before one another, and before the watching world, that tolerance of forced or institutional segregation based on race, and declarations of the inferiority of certain races, such as once were practiced and supported by our church and many other voices in the Presbyterian tradition, were wrong and cannot and will not be accepted within our church today or ever again. The Lord calls us to repent of the sin of prejudice; to turn from it and to treat all persons with justice, mercy, and love.[15]

This statement is an encouraging sign of real progress, especially if we see more Presbyterian church leaders and congregations throughout the southeastern United States make such courageous gospel confessions. These are great first steps for a church that still needs to deal with its own history for the sake of the gospel and for the sake of its own survival in an America that is increasingly becoming nonwhite.

The Event That Launched This Book

On Tuesday, November 3, 2009, Regent University announced Dr. Carlos Campo as its eighth president, filling the seat vacated by its founder, Dr. Pat Robertson, following news that Robertson would be stepping down from his duties at the school to become chancellor.[16] Universities acquiring new presidents are no big deal. It happens every year all over the country. What made the Regent announcement particularly significant was that a Latino leader was becoming the president of a major evangelical institution— perhaps the first Latino to assume such a role in US history. I was in shock, and I went on a search to find others. After searching for quite some time, I discovered that, while some evangelical colleges and seminaries may have blacks, Latinos, and Asian-Americans on the faculty or even in a few senior administrative positions, you will not find many black or Latino presidents among the evangelical schools accredited by the Association of Theological Schools and the evangelical member schools of the Council for Christian Colleges & Universities. In fact, the only other minority president of an accredited evangelical school in North America is the newly appointed Dr. Pete Menjares of Fresno Pacific University.[17] I wonder why it is that evangelical colleges and seminaries tend to be led by white males. What does this mean for a global Christianity where the center of growth is found neither in Europe nor in the United States, but in Africa, Asia, and Latin America? I wonder what impact this has on how Christian colleges and seminaries will raise up leaders for the church in the future. In fact, if evangelical institutions are going to have ethnic leaders, all levels of Christian life will need more diversity, from the local church to the seminary classroom.

Moving forward, evangelicals will need to learn how to partner and build relationships with predominately minority denominations that share the same commitments to the gospel and the authority of Scripture, but have not been traditionally considered "evangelical." For example, most evangelicals have never heard of the Church of God in Christ, which is the largest and most conservative black denomination in America, having nearly 5.5 million members.[18] I am wondering how resources and perspectives can be shared to bring greater unity to the body of Christ for the sake of the gospel (John 17). Many attempts have been made in the past few decades without much traction.

Diversify or Else?

In *The Next Evangelicalism: Freeing the Church from Western Cultural Captivity*, Soong-Chan Rah rocked the evangelical church by pointing out that, because of the realities of global Christianity, evangelicalism will become extinct in the United States if it does not begin to take race more seriously.[19] Rah uses the word *captivity* in the same way that Martin Luther used it to define cultural problems in Catholicism in his tract *On the Babylonian Captivity of the Church* (or in the way that R.C. Sproul wrote about the "Pelagian Captivity of the Church"). Using Rah's analysis, one would likely conclude that evangelical churches may be destined for continued decline unless Asians, Latin Americans, and communities connected to Africa and the Caribbean are handed the leadership baton, so that they offer direction. Rah wonders if evangelicalism's demise can be found in its cultural captivity to, and idolatrous worship of, white, Western cultural norms. For example, he points out that living in or near cities and not having multiethnic church leaders and members may be a recipe for extinction. In 1900, Europe and North America accounted for 82 percent of the world's Christian population. In 2005, that number is down to 39 percent. Presently, 60 percent of the world's Christians are in Africa, Asia, and Latin America. Moreover, by 2023 half of America's children will be nonwhite.[20] As these trends continue, America will likely have a white minority by 2050, observes Rah.[21]

Rah notes that, in the last fifty years, the evangelical church became enmeshed in secular values like individualism, consumerism, and materialism—and racism. According to Rah, evangelicals have turned Christianity into a "me-centered" faith, where one is concerned primarily with one's personal relationship with Jesus and one's own family, while ignoring the social dimensions of the gospel's work in local communities. Evangelicals tend to embrace a materialistic and consumerist expression of faith: families church hop to find the best youth programs or pursue the idols of comfort, ease, and professional success in comfortable church buildings.

Moreover, from the 1950s through 2000, evangelicalism grew significantly on the heels of "white flight" away from "liberals" and minorities. Suburban Christian schools grew. Suburban churches grew. Some churches even moved entire congregations out of cities to the suburbs to get away from minorities. Evangelicalism is so unaware of its syncretism and cultural captivity that the mere suggestion of its possibility is controversial.

Is Rah Right?

In 1994, I joined the Presbyterian Church in America (PCA). It remains a great denomination, committed to the historical, covenantal definition of *Reformed*, and I remain committed to it, flourishing with excitement for its future in global Christianity. Since its beginning, the PCA, like many evangelical denominations and associations, has appealed to white Christians who tend to be socially, politically, and theologically conservative within middle-class America, and the PCA is still highly successful at reaching that population. This is not a criticism, but simply an honest description of what it is. If denominations like the PCA do not diversify, what kind of future will they have?

Many wonder if the conservative evangelical captivity to white, Western culture will make it an outsider in a global Christian world that is primarily African, Asian, and Latin American. Using Soong-Chan Rah's book and the PCA, I conjectured about this on my blog in a post titled "Freeing the PCA from white, Western (and Southern) Cultural Captivity: A Rahian Analysis," which garnered lots of inadvertent attention.[22]

I simply wanted to set the stage for the application of Rah's analysis by first acknowledging the fact that global Christianity is no longer centered in Europe or North America. The center of global Christianity is now in Africa, Asia, and Latin America.[23] From Rah's perspective, evangelical churches remain primarily Eurocentric in their understanding of Christianity and how the gospel applies to modern life. Second, as America becomes increasingly nonwhite, predominantly white denominations will continue to stagnate or decline. Many suburban-centered confessional denominations experienced significant growth as a consequence of the white-flight cultural movement of the 1960s, 1970s, 1980s, and 1990s. But the homogenous unit principle that drove church planting during those decades can no longer produce the numbers that it used to.[24] Some call that era "planned apartheid."[25] But the initial white-flight movement has ended, and the once-celebrated homogeneity that grew the denomination may lead to its demise.

According to recent data, by 2023 half of America's children will be nonwhite. A church predominantly made up of white people is a church that will likely close its doors within the next generation. White-flight demographics cannot sustain confessional denominations in America's future because the growing and vibrant churches in America are primarily Asian, Latino, and immigrant churches.[26] Because ethnic denominations and associations are not a part of evangelicalism, they are often overlooked and ignored, leaving the impression that regions of the country (especially cities) are spiritually dead—when they are not. Finally, predominantly white evangelical denominations and associations have established a cultural context in which the only acceptable blacks, Latinos, and Asians are those who tend to be what some might call "sell-outs," "oreos," "twinkies," and the like—that is, those who are culturally white and tend to separate from their own ethnic communities. The more an ethnic person adopts white cultural norms, leaving his or her ethnic heritage behind and denigrating it, the more likely it is that that person will be embraced as a representative of "diversity" in evangelical circles.

Confusing racial tokenism with progress provides some denominations and associations with a false sense of progress.

To decorate agencies, committees, and staffs with racial minorities, as if they were ornaments on a Christmas tree, so as to give the *appearance* of progress, is unacceptable. These are *tokens*, people of color who are invited to strengthen existing systems and further the captivity of the dominant culture, says Rah.[27] There is a difference between being invited to sit on a committee as a token representative and being asked to lead the committee, staff, or agency, thus having whites submitting to the authority of people of color. Rah observes,

> The rules of the table have already been set and there's not a whole lot of room but come sit at our table. We won't change the way we interact with one another and we will need to maintain the white majority, but it still would be nice to have an Asian face or a black face to sit at our table. If the places at the table are already set, and ethnic minorities are asked to put aside their comfort to join an already existing power dynamic and structure, then we are not engaging in genuine ethnic diversity. Ethnic minorities are being asked to play the role of token minority who should be seen but not heard, rather than those who have wisdom and experience to transfer to the . . . community.[28]

Having an Asian, Latino, or black person sitting in a room, sitting on a committee, is different from ethnic members leading and determining future direction. This type of leadership transition requires whites to submit to the authority of nonwhites. For confessional denominations like the Reformed and Presbyterian churches, nonwhite leadership would be a new experience. Rah suggests that a denomination's understanding of the gospel and the kingdom is substandard, deficient, and handicapped unless it is also crafted by the theological contributions of Asians, Africans, and Latin Americans. We need new norms.

Virgilio Elizondo maintains, "Whites set the norms and project the image of success, achievement, acceptability, normalcy, and status."[29] There must be an honest conversation about how white privilege renders evangelical institutions incapable of having Asians, Latinos, African and Caribbean immigrants, and blacks as heads of agencies or chairing committees and determining direction, locally and globally.[30] White privilege maintains a system that places white culture in American society at the center and all other cultures on the fringes.[31] Socially nurtured in contexts of abundance, cultural dominance, and social ease, whites are by definition incapable of effectively applying the gospel to people whose stories arise out of poverty, suffering, and marginalization, suggests Rah.[32] When one's understanding of God emerges out of affluence and privilege, one's ability to relate and communicate to people who are not from that context is hindered. The cultural privilege that white Christians have had in America is foreign to the experience of Christians in the New Testament and the early church. Africans, Asians, Latinos, blacks, and Slavs in Eastern Europe, on the other hand, have a cultural experience more like that of the Christians in the early church, some argue.

Moving Forward

This book does not propose to provide all the solutions to the complex issue of race, but we do hope to show a way forward, to give those who care about diversity a framework for making needed changes. I was encouraged to say this in a discussion on race that was moderated by John Piper and Tim Keller in connection with Piper's book *Bloodlines*.[33] This book discusses the future of gospel-centered evangelicalism and its ability to reach diverse communities and raise up ethnic leaders who reflect the realities of global Christianity. The Lutheran Church—Missouri Synod (LCMS) has the best Protestant document to date that outlines what went wrong and explains the challenges that we face in the American context. In February

1994, the Commission on Theology and Church Relations of the LCMS released a report entitled "Racism and the Church." I included this document in the appendix because I believe it should serve as a representative starting point for all American Protestants for how to move forward. With clarity and honesty, the LCMS discusses why the Bible condemns racism, their own specific failings, theologically and ecclesiastically, the problem of white privilege, white flight, and paternalism, and the hard steps necessary for gospel-centered change in their denomination. I believe the Lutherans prophetically demonstrate good thinking and succeed at framing this discussion in ways that no evangelical has yet.

With the Lutheran document in hand, this book is intended to serve as a catalyst for a national conversation about moving forward. We do not have all the answers either, but the contributors to this volume intended to be fundamentally positive about the next steps. As shown by the previously mentioned email I received from a pastor, there are still some who believe that evangelicalism is immune to racism. So contributors begin their reflections with biographical accounts of their own encounters with racial tension within evangelicalism, but spend the bulk of their essays offering direction and hope for the future.

We begin with Rev. Lance Lewis, a pioneering African-American pastor in the Presbyterian Church in America, who reflects on the challenges of planting black churches in black communities, though the churches are in predominantly white denominations. Lewis describes ways in which church-planting initiatives can be more successful in reaching ethnic communities.

In chapter three, Dr. Amos Yong helps us understand some unique challenges among Asian-Americans in theological education. I searched for nearly two years to find Asian-American theologians who were willing and able to speak honestly. I asked several, and Dr. Yong was the only one who was able to join us. The project is enhanced by his contribution.

In chapter four, Dr. Juan Martínez writes about developing Hispanic pastoral leadership. He focuses on the unique challenges of planting churches in Hispanic communities and developing Hispanic pastoral influence in predominantly white denominations. Dr. Martínez has been developing Hispanic leaders for decades, and his wisdom and experience are invaluable.

In chapter five, Dr. Vincent Bacote writes on the challenges of blacks and Latinos in publishing within evangelical theological associations, paying special attention to the Evangelical Theological Society. Dr. Bacote is a seasoned theologian with commitments to developing space for minorities to make contributions to evangelical discourse.

In chapter six, Dr. Harold Dean Trulear focuses on the challenges of recruiting and developing blacks and Latinos in academic, teaching, and leadership positions in predominantly white Christian colleges and seminaries. Some readers may be unfamiliar with Dr. Trulear and his work at Howard University. He has been a leader in the National Association of Black Evangelicals for several years and is a fellow at the Center for Public Justice. Dr. Trulear has volunteered and consulted for a number of organizations, such as InterVarsity Christian Fellowship and Biblical Theological Seminary.

Dr. Orlando Rivera writes in chapter seven on the challenges of recruiting, graduating, training, and placing blacks and Latinos in Christian colleges and seminaries. Professor Rivera has special expertise in the church, theological education, and organizational management.

In chapter eight, we get perspective from someone in a traditionally black denomination. Dr. Ralph C. Watkins offers a black church perspective on minorities in predominantly white institutions. This chapter focuses on ways in which predominantly white

Christian institutions have partnered with historically black denominations. Watkins is an evangelical who has remained in the African Methodist Episcopal Church, a traditionally black denomination.

Finally, we round out the book with a chapter on application. Dr. Carl Ellis Jr. provides an example of what it looks like to apply the principles mentioned by the contributors to the discipling of men from low-income contexts at the church level. Dr. Ellis has labored for years in the Presbyterian Church in America for the cause of racial solidarity and has been an important mentor for me on these matters. I am delighted to include a model of how much these discussions matter on the ground.

It is our hope that readers will engage this book critically by taking the contributors' personal stories seriously and reflecting publicly with us on what is best for the future. What we all have in common is a desire for the kingdom to manifest itself in the life of the church through dependence on the grace of God and a desire for the Holy Spirit to move as evangelicals embrace new opportunities for the sake of the gospel and the glory of God.

2

Black Pastoral Leadership
and Church Planting

Lance Lewis

"TOTO, I HAVE A FEELING we're not in Kansas anymore."[1]
That about sums up my feelings upon entering an evangelical church for the first time with the intention of becoming a
member. I had previously had some contact with evangelicals
and their organizations, heard them on the radio, and even been
to a few of their churches. Yet that's how I felt as I crossed the
threshold into a different world. And a different world it was.
Now I didn't intend to become part of an evangelical denomination or part of the evangelical subculture. At that point in my
life, I had embraced certain aspects of evangelical doctrine that
made it necessary to leave the Pentecostal church of which I had
been a member for several years. Beyond that, I had developed a
strong conviction and desire for more consistent teaching from
the pulpit and was convinced that an evangelical church was the
place to meet that need. It was not my intention to take a walk

through the looking glass, and there have been many times when I have questioned that decision.

The Good—Preaching and People

So why did I stay? That's a long story for another book. Suffice it to say that the evangelical church held certain attractions to a young black man who had grown dissatisfied and disillusioned with certain aspects of the black church. It was similar to how many black children were drawn to the Brady Bunch. There was something intriguing about watching this kind of family, even though they certainly didn't look like, speak like, or live like we did. I was attracted to, and still appreciate that part of, the evangelical church that values expository preaching. God speaks through his Word. Moreover, constant and consistent preaching through the books and major themes of God's Word presents his people with the proper vision of God in all his glory, holiness, beauty, majesty, and sovereignty, as fully expressed in Jesus Christ. It is vitally important that the people of God love, desire, and pursue the living God as an end in itself. Preaching that mainly focuses on my issues, my dreams, my problems, and my potential is in the end an exercise in idolatry. Preaching that lifts its themes from the text of Scripture is preaching that can highlight the main point, theme, plot, and story of Scripture, which is the person and work of Jesus Christ. I was attracted to and still value those within the evangelical tradition who hold to this practice.

Another good thing about the evangelical church is something it has in common with most all other churches, and that is its people. I've made many dear friends and am grateful to have shared my life with them. And that's important. All too often we criticize the church as if it were merely an institution with flaws and shortcomings. Although the church is an organization, it is also a family of people. Many of these people come to know, love, rejoice, and mourn with us. Does the church have its shortcomings? Of course it does, but so do you. And, truth be told, you probably haven't been the best example of a believer who has ever set foot on the planet. Thus, as we highlight some of the deficiencies of the evangelical church, be sure to remember that, like other churches, it has its strength, and much of that strength consists of good, sincere, and godly people who, like the rest of us, are in the process of working out their own salvation.

The Bad

In highlighting the bad, it's important to keep in mind that I'm defining or categorizing something as being bad inasmuch as it either hinders or works directly against the church's commission to proclaim the gospel of Jesus Christ and live out the convictions associated with that gospel. This is the church's chief mission, and thus anything and everything that in any way hinders or opposes that mission must be checked, addressed, and stopped. Moreover, lest we become arrogant, it's necessary to realize that this kind of "bad" is within every church and every believer. Thus, the point of addressing these issues now is not to look askance at the evangelical church, but to lovingly point it in the direction of the gospel's witness.

So here goes. More than twenty years of experience within the evangelical church has shown me that its focus on conservative politics is bad, in that it competes with our witness and, at times, even replaces our main mission. Now let's be clear. I am not in any way saying that having conservative political convictions, acting on such convictions, and having strong feelings about those convictions is wrong. However, my experience within the church has shown me that an undue focus and emphasis on those convictions is bad for the church because they hinder our witness, can cause serious division, and confuse our main purpose. Far too often I've been in situations where people conveyed—and sometimes openly declared—that biblical faith was synonymous with conservative political ideology. In fact, years ago I responded to a letter to the editor that emphatically expressed the conviction that anyone who dared to vote for Bill Clinton could not be a Christian. I've been a part of far too many conversations in which, if I didn't know any better, it would appear that conservative political convictions are the substance of the faith once delivered to the saints, that our fellowship—i.e., that which we hold in common—was our affiliation with the conservative wing of the Republican Party, and that the mission into which we should pour our lives and souls was the promotion and preservation of the supremacy of the United States. Once more, my issue isn't with conservative politics, but with how they're held on to and expressed within the evangelical church, to the extent that they have actually become a test of orthodoxy and replace the church's mission to make active followers of Jesus Christ from all peoples.

The Ugly

Every church, whether an individual congregation or a denomination, as well as every person, has some ugly within. The ugly goes beyond the bad by being an actual rebellion against, and repudiation of, the living God, our Lord Jesus Christ, and the gospel that bears his name. It is ugly in that we allow it to have a hold over us, and in our arrogance actually defend it with "biblical proof." My time within certain parts of the evangelical church has revealed that the ugliness of racism still resides among some of us. By *racism* I mean the unbiblical and ungodly conviction that certain groups of people are not only different, but in some way inferior and less desirable than others, coupled with the conviction that certain other groups are more pure and godly. It hurts me to say that a pastor who confronted a blatant act of racism was actually challenged and confronted by the regional group of pastors to which he was accountable within his denomination's governmental structure. It hurts me to know that a pastor who came to his defense was eventually forced out of his congregation because of "his undue focus on dealing with racism." It's both shocking and ugly to know that ordained ministers within evangelical churches actually believe that one can hold racist views simply as a matter of conscience, and they need not or should not be confronted and disciplined for the expression of such racism.

Moving Forward: Church Planting, Why Not?

By God's grace, I've spent the last sixteen years directly involved in church planting for an evangelical denomination. During this time, I've served three church plants, including a congregation I planted, and have spent countless hours praying, thinking, talking, and learning about church planting. All that experience has taught me a thing or two, which I'm happy to share with those evangelicals interested in church planting among black folks. My advice, you ask? In short, it's this: don't do it. And, yes, I mean that. I'm not being sarcastic or trying to set you up for a don't-do-it-unless-you-intend-to-do-it-the-right-way rant. All of my experiences and observations have shown me that evangelicals need to stay away from church planting among black people the way a toddler needs to stay away from a fork and an electric outlet.

Why so drastic? Here are a few reasons to begin with. First, the whole premise of evangelicals specifically targeting black people (and, for the most part, dependently poor black people) is, frankly, arrogant. It's arrogant because the assumption is that there are no "good" churches in black neighborhoods that could possibly meet the spiritual needs of the community in the same way that an evangelical church could. Trust me, I grew up in a poor black neighborhood (I think they call them "inner-city" neighborhoods now) and was never more than a block and a half away from a church. I specifically remember hearing the gospel clearly from my grandmother, who was a faithful member of the neighborhood Pentecostal church. Moreover, I distinctly recall the times my older cousin took me to a evangelistic street outreach given by Deliverance Evangelistic Church under the leadership of the late Dr. Benjamin Smith. And I remember the night a friend came to take me to National Temple Church of the Living God, where Bishop Raymond White was running a revival. And guess what? He preached the gospel of Christ crucified and the need for faith in him for forgiveness of sin and new life. And though the mainstream, dominant culture may be trending more secular, the same is not true for the majority of African-Americans. All it takes is a brief drive or walk through a black community to see the number of churches it boasts. It would be impossible for any evangelical denomination or ministry to plant a church in an all-black community that doesn't already have several active congregations serving that community. Since that's true, one must ask the question: why have we decided to plant here? The unspoken answer is: the existing black churches just aren't very good.

Second, to this day most evangelicals know very little about African-Americans, have little real contact with them, and, like most people in dominant societies, truly believe that their way is the best and only way. This lack of knowledge leads to evangelical denominations projecting their own misinformed views onto black people on the assumption that they (evangelicals) know what's best for blacks, their families, and their communities. Does ignorance automatically mean that evangelicals shouldn't seek to plant churches among black people? Not necessarily, but given my first reason (the many churches already there), it is one more reason to resist the urge to ride to the rescue of the black community. The black community has had over four hundred years to grow, cultivate, and enjoy a particular and unique church culture. Do we really think that they're just going to give that up because evangelicals show up and say, "Okay, we're here, now we can really start doing church right"?

The third reason is somewhat related to the second. To put it bluntly, black people don't trust evangelicals. It was evangelicals who not only closed their churches, but also their hearts, during the height of the Civil Rights Movement. "Hold it, that was nearly fifty years ago; what happened to forgive and forget?" The issue is not one of forgiveness, but one of trust. The truth is that, for most black folks, evangelicals have not in any way, shape, or form demonstrated that they have our best interests in mind or at heart. To give an example, I'd like to cite the Republican Party's 2008 presidential convention—particularly the speech given by vice presidential candidate Sarah Palin. I made a point to watch the speech, and I can tell you that her tone, rhetoric, and substance made it clear to me that we (that is, black people who live in poor communities) were not the kind of "Americans" she was interested in reaching out to or serving. "Preposterous! She didn't say anything about African-Americans." I know, but I can tell you that most black folks I know would have had the same reaction to her speech. "But I don't understand." I know—as I said, you just don't know us, and we do not trust you.

A fourth reason why evangelicals should call a moratorium on church planting among black people is that black evangelical leaders (including yours truly) are out of touch and would have almost as much, and perhaps more, trouble connecting with the black community as do white evangelical leaders. Now I know that might surprise you, but it's true. As we African-Americans migrated from traditional black churches into evangelical churches and ministries, we gradually lost touch with our communities. Try as we may, we rarely regain that connection.

The fact that a man has a black face and comes from a black church doesn't mean that he'll be able to connect with black people. His preaching, which seems dynamic and out of sight to you, may be viewed as odd and irrelevant to the community of his birth. I don't know how many times I've commiserated with black evangelical pastors over African-Americans who like us and admire our integrity, but who just can't connect with our preaching. That's not to say that all that black people will listen to is traditional black preaching. My experience, however, is that they will not become members or active attendees of a church that features mainstream evangelical teaching as its primary form of preaching.

A fifth and final reason to refrain from church planting among African-Americans is motive. Just why do evangelical denominations and organizations want to plant churches in poor black communities? I'm asking about those communities because, for the most part, I've not heard the call to plant churches among middle-income blacks who live in the suburbs. The stock answer to that question usually has something to do with black people needing to hear the gospel. But what makes you think that black people don't have the opportunity to hear the gospel from the existing churches within their community? Once more, my experience with evangelicals has taught me that, for the most part, they completely dismiss the black churches in African-American communities. I distinctly recall a conversation in which a colleague declared with confidence that a certain evangelical church of several hundred members was the largest church in a particular area. But I knew that wasn't true because there were at least two black churches of several thousand members in that area. So, once more, what's the reason—and I mean the real reason—behind the standard evangelical rhetoric? To be clear, I'm not saying that there are no valid reasons. However, those reasons must be defined and examined thoroughly before a church makes this kind of commitment.

Plan B

"Okay, I kind of hear what you're saying, but here's the problem: telling a denomination to refrain from church planting is like telling Ford to stop building cars. Church planting is what we do, and if we're not going to use our newly found black ministers to plant churches among black people, then what in the world will they do?"

Good question. As I continue to try to answer it, let me remind you that all my experience with evangelicals has been with one denomination, so it may not translate directly to others. Still, from what I hear and understand, the similarities are pretty close.

The denomination I serve is an ecclesiastical organization. Because we're an evangelical ecclesiastical organization, our mission (or reason for being) is to promote the gospel of Jesus Christ. Thus, we believe that the Scriptures are actually the word of God; that Jesus, though he has always existed, was born of the Virgin Mary; that he lived a sinless life, performed authentic miracles, taught about the kingdom of God to the people of first-century Palestine, was crucified, actually died on the cross, was buried, and then physically rose from the grave. After showing himself to his closest followers for about a month and a half, he went back to heaven and has promised to return to end human history, judge the world, and forever live with his people in the new heavens and new earth.

However, though we're an ecclesiastical organization, we function like a for-profit corporation. By that I mean that we, like other corporations, seek to increase our market share. To put it straight, we don't engage in evangelism so that those whom God saves will go to other evangelical churches. And, though we start churches with the intent of filling them with the unconverted, we will gladly accept transfers from other evangelical denominations. Before you get too cynical, I'm not saying this as a knock on evangelicals. Almost every evangelical, Bible-believing church I know of that engages in outreach does so, at least in part, to add to its numbers. Now, just as most corporations seek to increase their market share, most take some time to divide their potential market into various groups. They do this to maximize their resources, so as to get the most from their investment in a particular group. That's why you won't see a Starbucks in most poor black communities. Does that mean that Starbucks is an evil, racist company? Of course not. It merely means that it has made a business decision regarding its product and believes that it will do best in neighborhoods that aren't mainly poor, whether black or white. On the other hand, Dunkin' Donuts has decided that setting up shop in poor black neighborhoods works for it, and so, as they say, "The 'hood runs on Dunkin'."

Well, like company, like church. My denomination and, I suppose, others like it go through the process of dividing their potential market into various groups for the purpose of deciding on which groups they will invest their church-planting capital, both men and money. For the last twenty years or so, the evangelical church has been enthralled with the *Seinfeld/Friends* market. That is, it has sought to reach those white, educated professionals who have settled in the central areas of large cities.

Evangelicals have fastened their attention and focused their resources on capturing this prized market—and for good reason. Many of these people are the children of evangelical baby boomers who were reared in, and became disenchanted with, their parents' church. The evangelical focus on this group doesn't mean that they have completely abandoned their core market of politically conservative, middle-income suburbanites. This group still commands a share of the attention and investment, though at least for now it must play second fiddle to the new urban hipsters. Where does that leave African-Americans?

38

For now, they're at least a distant third—and perhaps even fourth, behind our Hispanic brothers and sisters, in terms of investment.

To give you an example, according to its statistics, one evangelical denomination had about three hundred church plants in 2009. Of these, about 3 percent were targeted to African-Americans. Moreover, this denomination is looking to target several other communities across the country, none of which have a black population of more than 20 percent, with most having less than 5 percent. Once more, does this indicate a streak of evil racism within this denomination? No, it most certainly does not. It indicates where it has invested its church-planting resources in the past and where it intends to invest them in the near future. For the most part, black folks just don't figure in that equation.

"But wait," you say. "Perhaps they would target communities with more black folks if the black evangelical ministers led the way." Although that sounds reasonable, the facts (as per my experience) just don't bear that out. Remember what I said about market share. For now, white urban hipsters are the Holy Grail to most evangelical denominations. They're followed by the tried-and-true, middle-income, suburbanite crew. Consequently, if and when blacks show up, they must wait at the back of the line. You may recall telling your children that they could either spend a quarter in the candy machine or the toy machine at the supermarket. They had to make a choice, since you can't spend the same quarter twice. It's roughly the same with church-planting resources. While most evangelical denominations would affirm the desire to plant congregations in black communities, their dollars say otherwise. Trust me, I'm very well aware of this. I, as well as a number of other black church planters whom I know, have felt the sting of struggling to raise funds and hitting the field with the bare minimum to get started. We did so against all wisdom because of our sincere desire to bring the gospel to our people.

Here are just a couple of examples to illustrate this sad and distressing reality. Before planting my present congregation, I attended the various church-planting training events sponsored by my denomination. At one such event, we went through an exercise in constructing the church budget. The budget covered salary, worship space expense, various ministry expenses, outreach expense, and so on. If I recall correctly, the average budget at that time was about $125,000. We were told that this exercise was important because we needed sufficient funds to get the church plant off to the right start. After returning home from the conference, I began constructing a budget using the template and categories provided in my church-planting manual. For some reason, my budget came in at about fifteen to twenty thousand dollars less than the sample budget, so I was pretty giddy about contacting the denomination's church-planting arm to discuss it and ways we could begin to raise the money. Much to my shock and dismay, I was told that my budget was entirely too high and was considered a "blue-sky budget." Additionally, I was informed that I had to figure out the bare minimum needed to begin this work that specifically targeted black people. Think about that for a moment. I was the lone black church planter in a major American city, in a denomination that wanted to serve a geographical area that contained over one million black people. At that time, my denomination had no black churches of any kind anywhere near this area. And it was telling me to go in and represent it with the bare minimum of resources! And, like an idiot, I did. I began this outreach to the black people in a major metropolitan area with little more than my salary.

There are other horror stories, but one more will suffice. I have a good friend who also went through the same process to plant a church targeting the black community of a major metropolitan area. He was told in no uncertain terms that completing a church-planting evaluation was the key to raising funds for his plant, and that this was critical since he was such an unknown in the denomination. He completed the evaluation with an approved rating and, after inquiring as to how to get started, was stonewalled. Once again an eager black man who believed in both his God and *his denomination's professed desire to take the gospel to all peoples* was left to start a church in a costly area with little more than his salary.

I've shared this to make two general points with respect to how evangelical denominations ought to utilize their African-American ministers in light of my conviction that they should not be used in church planting. First, as I said before, evangelical denominations need to call a moratorium on church planting among black people. My experience has shown that, in addition to the reasons I listed in the first section, evangelicals have not been willing to devote the necessary resources to church planting. And the result is that many good men travel an excruciating, gut-wrenching road once they take the path to church planting among their people. Second, to those eager, passionate, loyal, and dedicated black men who so enthusiastically embrace evangelical doctrine and culture with the intention of going back to their community and transforming them with the gospel: *Don't drink the Kool-Aid!* The best way you can be of service to your newly adopted faith community is either to take an existing evangelical congregation and faithfully serve them or to take on a church-planting project that is *not* targeted at black people. By the time you have gone through seminary (during which you no doubt attended an evangelical church), you have not only learned its theology, but also embraced its conservative politics (not a negative, just a fact) and its cultural norms, so you are probably no longer able to connect with the community of your birth as you once could. However, your gifts, personality, training, and passion will suit you very well in the average evangelical setting. There's a reason why those evangelicals like your preaching so much and swear you're the next Tony Evans. Many of them would be eager to sit under your preaching and follow your pastoral leadership, and you should take them up on that.

Now, you could ignore my warning and take up your own personal charge of the Light Brigade, and that's your choice. But I ask you to consider my words, if only for the sake of your family. Perhaps you're in a situation in which you're ministering to a niche group in the greater black community, so much of what I've written may not apply. It's just that I've seen far too many good men crash on the rocks of their broken church-planting dreams, only to see their denomination look the other way and hope not to hear from them again. The spiritual, emotional, and psychological toll is devastating. Some cannot recover, and they leave the ministry altogether. And their families suffer with them.

Is there a way to follow your passion to serve your people and at the same time engage in ministry that in the long run is wiser and healthier for you and your family? Yes, I believe there is. Several years ago I began a fellowship with a number of other black evangelical pastors. This fellowship has now matured to the point that we have taken some direct action (not church planting) to engage African-Americans, hoping that in time we'll be able to serve them more directly. It's my view that this is the wisest way for evangelical denominations and their African-American ministers to impact the greater black community. No, it's not as sexy as church planting, but, given time and persistence, it can pay out significant dividends. It involves hosting events that speak to the chief concerns of the greater black community in settings where there is no pressure on them to convert to the evangelical cause. This ministry is vital in that it meets our need to serve our community without the potential sacrifice of the spiritual, emotional, and psychological health of ourselves and our families. It also allows evangelical denominations to continue their focus on their primary markets while participating in substantive ministry to black people, and does so at a fraction of the cost of church planting.

Am I forever ruling out evangelicals planting churches within black communities? No, I'm not. But they should not do so unless and until they answer the why question honestly and begin to address the other concerns I previously mentioned. And please understand that I'm not questioning the sincerity of those evangelicals who truly wish to see greater communal unity across ethnic lines. I am writing from my experience, which I know is also the experience of many other black evangelicals.

Oh, and about the church plants I mentioned. As I said, my denomination didn't have a single black congregation in a metro area of over one million African-Americans ten years ago. Now it has one served by yours truly and, as far as I know, it has no plans to begin another. And my friend, well, he did his level best for seven years, but with little or no help and after suffering extreme spiritual, emotional, and psychological exhaustion, he finally listened to words of wisdom and left for a pastorate at an established church. The church plant folded.

3

RACE AND RACIALIZATION IN A POST-RACIST EVANGELICALISM: A VIEW FROM ASIAN AMERICA

Amos Yong

THE TITLE of this chapter, especially the "post-racist" reference, is loaded.[1] Although it appears to grant that evangelicals live in a post-racist world—at least in the sense that racism is illegal in this country—it also asserts that there are (strong) undercurrents of racialization that persist. By *racialization* I mean the social processes of devaluing nonwhite ethnicity and culture, of subordinating the latter to the dominant white regime, and, in some cases, even seeking to eliminate such from the contemporary cultural landscape.[2] Let me be clear: I believe that the North American evangelical world has taken many important steps toward overcoming the racist history of slavery in this country, and my own story, to be told in this chapter, reflects how I and other Asian-Americans have been beneficiaries of such repentant attitudes and even practices. Simultaneously, it would be a mistake for us to think that simply because we now live in an era of equal opportunity and celebrate America as a multicultural society, race is no longer an issue and that evangelicals are neither affected by nor complicit in the ongoing processes of racialization. This chapter provides perspectives on both sides of this post-racist and yet still racialized reality from the perspective of an Asian-American evangelical theologian. The first part of what follows unfolds through an interweaving of personal and theological reflections.[3] The second part suggests how a still predominantly white North American evangelical establishment might continue and expand the work of racial reconciliation.

Race, Racialization, and Racism in Evangelicalism: A Slanted (Asian) Perspective

I cannot speak for all Asian-Americans. There are too many differences from South Asia (India) to East Asia (Korea and Japan), not to mention from North Asia (Mongolia and China) to Southeast and Southern Asia (Malaysia, Singapore, and Indonesia) and to the Pacific Rim (the Philippines).[4] I therefore give what I call a "slanted," or biased, perspective,[5] obviously playing off my phenotypical features as a Malaysian-born, Chinese immigrant to the USA. Yet the following is not to be read merely autobiographically. As a Pentecostal theologian, I believe that our testimonies are also modes of witness that declare the wondrous works of God for his glory (Acts 2:11). Hence, the following weaves together personal and theological considerations.

I was born in Muslim-controlled Malaysia in the same year (1965) that America passed the Immigration Act, opening the door for massive migration from Asian countries and elsewhere. Yet even before leaving for America, I was racialized in a complex, multicultural society. As a person of Chinese descent, I belonged to a minority in a Muslim-dominated nation that had only just achieved independence from the British a few years before (in 1957). Malaysia was thus an emerging postcolonial state, struggling to finds its own way in the modernizing world. I had to learn Malay, the national language, and English (British English, to be precise) during my first few years of elementary public school education, but that meant that I had no opportunity to learn how to speak Chinese, except with my grandparents, whenever they visited or we visited them. The Malaysian Chinese thus experienced racism both from their Muslim rulers and through the legacy of the colonial enterprise.

My parents were first-generation converts to Christianity through the ministry of Pentecostal Assemblies of God (AG) missionaries from the USA. My father trained for the ministry and had a congregation before I was born, so I grew up as a Pentecostal "preacher's kid." Because it was against the law to proselytize and evangelize Muslims, our Pentecostal churches were predominantly Chinese (who make up about 25 percent of the Malaysian population), with a very small number of people of South Indian ancestry (about 7 percent of the overall Malaysian population). I will be forever grateful for the American missionaries under whose labors my parents and I became Christians and grew in our faith. However, they also bequeathed to us a racialized view of the world, about which I will say more in a moment.

In 1975, my parents received an invitation from one of the AG missionaries to Malaysia, whose burden for Chinese-speaking peoples led her to plant churches for immigrants from Hong Kong and southern China in her home state of California. To oversee these churches, she sponsored the immigration of a number of Malaysian pastors to California. My parents were among those who came. I now became a "missionary kid" to the USA and part of the earliest wave of what missiologists call "reverse mission" from the Global South to the Western world.[6]

I first experienced the overt realities of American racism during my junior high school years in the San Joaquin Valley of California. I stood out, not only because I had slanted eyes and a foreign accent, but also because I, as part of a missionary family supported by the AG district's (low) "home missions" budget—my parents called it "living by faith"—wore hand-me-downs that the sponsoring (white) churches collected and gave to us each Christmas. On a few occasions, I almost got into fights because I resented being called a "chink." I worked hard during these years, not only dealing with adolescence, but also ridding myself of my Malaysian-Chinese accent. I still get comments like, "Oh, I thought you were born here; you don't sound like a foreigner." Now (as of the time of writing) I am enrolled in a first-year college Chinese course and am doing my best to speak Chinese "right"! Is it too late to undo what was done?

When I was in junior high school, my wrestling-with-identity issues prompted a series of discussions with my parents, especially my father. I wanted to know what my culture was. Was I Malaysian, Chinese, American, or some kind of hybrid? My father said I did not have to worry about cultural aspects of my identity; since we were Christians, we were culturally Christian. I accepted this answer at that time, but I have since learned that it was typical of the thinking of AG missionaries, pastors, and church leaders during the middle quarters of the twentieth century. Of course, the AG also belonged to a wider North American Pentecostal and evangelical world, and such ideas were just as prominent there as well. The point was that Christianity was characterized by North American cultural habits, and converts to Christianity were expected to leave behind their cultural traditions in turning to Christ. What they were not told—because it was not even understood as such by the missionaries—was that turning to Christ involved embracing the culture of the missionaries also.[7] There were subtle and more obvious ways in which this "truth" was communicated. Nevertheless, my father "got it," and he passed it on to me when I inquired. Such a racialized self-understanding followed me for many more years.

It turned out that during my high school years, from which I graduated as one of six valedictorians (with two other Asians!), I fit the stereotype of Asians as "model minority" immigrants to America.[8] This, however, is unfair on at least three counts. It is unfair to Asians, since there is a diversity of Asian cultures, with a range of work and other habits. Why should we measure all ethnic and cultural Asians by norms attained by only some of them? It is also unfair to other immigrants and people of color, especially African-Americans, since that suggests that they are of an inferior type or quality when compared to Asians. Last, but not least, it is unfair to all Americans, period: stereotypes raise hopes, and incorrect stereotypes set everyone up for failed expectations. Judging people by their skin color or their looks is a form of racism; the repetition of stereotypes about "model minorities" perpetuates racialization in a supposedly post-racist world.

I went to Bethany College in California—a school founded in the Bible institute tradition of classical Pentecostalism—for my undergraduate studies to prepare for what I felt God calling me to: Christian ministry. From there I went on to get a master's degree in the history of Christianity from Western Evangelical Seminary (now part of George Fox University) in the Wesleyan-Holiness tradition, and then a second master's in intellectual history from Portland State University, a secular institution—both in the Portland, Oregon, area. My studies were thoroughly Western. I do not recall having any teachers or professors of color, and the curriculum was dominated by Anglo-American perspectives. Bethany, as a denominationally affiliated school, inculcated the values and ethos of the AG and also wider North American evangelicalism in students.

Western Seminary introduced me to the broader Western Christian tradition (I actually wrote my master's thesis on the reception of the Chalcedonian doctrine of the two natures of Christ in the West), and Portland State immersed me into the Western canon of "great books." I do not recall much discussion of race. It was as if race realities did not exist. Yet not talking about race itself has allowed the subterranean streams of racialization to continue flowing. In any case, even in such a white world, I still managed to meet and marry a Mexican-American fellow student at Bethany, and, with that, my racialized identity doubled in its complexity. I return to this part of the story in a moment.

I should note that I first encountered the non-Western world during my coursework at Portland through a philosophy professor who had us read the philosophy of Alfred North Whitehead (1861–1947), whose ideas continue to be well-received internationally. It was there that I learned of the growing dialogue between Western and Eastern philosophers, striving toward articulation of what is called "world philosophy." I began then to observe that there were similar trends afoot in theological circles, especially mainline Protestant and Roman Catholic, about the importance of engaging with Eastern or Asian perspectives even in theology. All this was part of my doctoral course of study at Boston University in the mid-1990s.[9] Although the Western philosophical and theological tradition was still the starting point for much of what we studied at Boston, there were also intentional efforts to register the perspectives of women and people of color and to engage with ethnic, cultural, philosophical, and religious traditions in the Global South.

Not too long after completing my Ph.D. at Boston, I landed a theology position at Bethel University in St. Paul, Minnesota. I worked there and thrived for six years. A department chair that recognized the need to diversify the theology faculty welcomed me, and I found nothing but support from the wider faculty and Bethel administration. This does not mean that Bethel was exempt from the racialized realities of North American evangelicalism. Bethel is affiliated with the Baptist General Conference (BGC), a pietist denomination with deep roots in the Swedish immigration to the Upper Midwest region of the USA in the mid-nineteenth century. My blond-haired, blue-eyed Scandinavian students put up with me while I learned how to talk about the importance of "global perspectives." Theologically, the BGC considers itself broadly evangelical, and certainly sees itself as contributing to the discussion of what it means to be evangelical in the twenty-first century. As a Chinese-American Pentecostal theologian, I found myself thrust into a set of discussions, even debates, carried out mostly by exercised white evangelicals.[10] Culturally, it was at Bethel that I experienced for the first time what my father said, but in a way that he did not mean. Conversion to Christianity did bring with it a conversion to Christian culture at some level; the only thing is that in the Upper Midwest such "Christian culture" takes on a very white form of life.

Our family moved in 2005, when I joined the faculty at Regent University in Virginia. After having lived on the West Coast and in the Northeast and Upper Midwest, we finally experienced in a more palpable way the stain of the long history of slavery when we arrived in this northernmost of the Southern states. Service workers remain largely African-Americans in this part of the country, and there would probably be more people of color in these occupations if it were not that the demographics in the Commonwealth of Virginia are largely black and white. Yet my colleagues at Regent are committed to an inclusive vision of the coming reign of God. Charismatic evangelical minister, entrepreneur, and one-time presidential aspirant M. G. "Pat"

Robertson founded Regent in the late 1970s, and he has always had a heart for the Chinese people. Our new president (as of 2010) is a Cuban-American who is committed to engaging the Hispanic world. Our faculty, at least in the School of Divinity, where I am located, strives to engage students with a global vision, which includes heeding the voices and perspectives of women and people of color.

While I feel quite accepted at Regent, my African-American colleagues still face racist attitudes and even harassment. I wonder sometimes if being Asian in what for some is still a starkly black-and-white American South protects me to some degree. I also wonder if people will like me less if I begin to write and speak more intentionally about racism and racialization.[11] Perhaps I am "safe" because I have earned my academic stripes, so to speak, by talking about matters that do not set in relief the underlying realities of race in what we would like to think is a post-racist world.

By now, of course, I have become quite comfortable in the racialized world that I inhabit. After all, I occupy a named chair and have some degree of influence as director of the Ph.D. program here at my institution. My dean and my colleagues seem to appreciate my work. To be sure, my children have interesting questions about whether they should embrace more the Chinese or the Mexican aspects of their identity, and they usually figure out that there are advantages to being able to claim either, depending on the situation.[12] They certainly inhabit and benefit from the cultural styles of middle-class America in ways that their parents never did growing up. Are not my family and I examples of the dawn of a post-racist North American culture and evangelicalism? That is certainly the mantra of the dominant (white) culture: that regardless of one's skin color, all one has to do is to work hard to attain the American dream. Is that what it is all about in the end?

Moving Forward toward a Post-Racist Evangelicalism

In light of the preceding discussion, I now want to outline what I feel are the most important next steps with regard to shaping a post-racist evangelicalism. I will frame my remarks at the level of what I call the conscientization of evangelical culture more generally and then address ecclesial concerns and theological education issues. Again, these remarks are informed only by my limited Asian-American perspective. Other Asian-Americans have made and will make other proposals, and certainly other persons of color have important insights to register.

Transforming Evangelical Culture

Although American culture is not monolithic, there is strong pressure on people of color to assimilate to the American way of life. Yet this overlooks the forces of globalization and transnationalization that impinge on all Americans, especially on Asian-Americans and their communities. While there are generations of Asian-Americans who have roots in this country prior to 1965, the post-1965 influx of immigrants (legal and undocumented), refugees, and exiles from across the Pacific Ocean has forever transformed the face of Asian America. More and more Asian-Americans, including citizens, have a global consciousness. American evangelical culture needs to awaken to the dynamic global and transnational character of evangelicalism.[13] On the one hand, this involves recognizing the diversity of evangelical sensibilities, commitments, and forms of life around the world. On the other hand, some old racist and racializing habits will have to be left behind. None of this ought to threaten the core of the gospel, but, as I will indicate in a moment, it might require that North American evangelicals become more flexible and open to engaging in discussions about how to understand the Christian faith in a global context.

North American evangelical conscientization ought to involve taking a hard look at the processes of racialization that have been and are in place in our culture. There are pressures that Asian-Americans and other people of color face personally, in work places, in schools, and in other social venues to conform to the American way of life. Part of the problem is that Americanization often involves certain negative value judgments about other cultures, languages, and practices that result in the perpetuation of racist attitudes even in the post-racist world that we aspire to inhabit. Evangelical churches can continue to acquiesce to such racializing modalities of culture or can, perhaps for the first time, prophetically resist them. To take up the latter, evangelical organizations, networks, and parachurch groups might consider engaging in a process of conscientization for the common good, not only of evangelicals, but of American culture as a whole. Should not evangelicals be at the forefront of thinking about deconstructing the dynamics of racialization if we are truly serious about a post-racist society? Why do evangelicals usually only react to more secular injunctions to reform, like the Civil Rights Movement, when we should be in the lead? Perhaps there is a need for evangelicals to look deeply into and confront their history of colonialism, Anglo-Americanism, and racism;[14] it takes great courage to be honest about such matters.

Transforming Evangelical Churches

None of the preceding disappears when we descend from the broader culture to the level of evangelical churches. In fact, the intensity of the pressure to assimilate increases. Most Asian-American evangelicals live "betwixt and between," caught outside two worlds, neither fully Asian nor fully American.[15] Theirs is what might be called a liminal experience, always in the process of becoming something else that may gain certain benefits— i.e., acceptance by American culture and evangelicalism as a whole—but ends up losing other aspects of tradition, culture, and language that are regretted in the long run.[16] As I have already suggested, such pressure persists, however subtly, even within evangelical Christianity.

Asian-Americans have attempted to navigate such racializing processes in a variety of ways. For newer immigrants, of course, the initial ethnic church provides an environment of support, enabling adjustment in a foreign land. Yet such churches, usually within a span of a few years, if not a decade, are forced to face up to the challenges of assimilation in light of their children's experiences. Second- and third-generation children find themselves either completely absorbed by the dominant culture (white churches) or form pan-Asian communities of faith. Many megachurches in major urban areas with large Asian-American populations are increasingly pan-Asian or simply multicultural to a greater or lesser degree. Yet the predominantly white leadership of mega-churches often has little perspective on the issues with which Asian-Americans are burdened. Where will the resources come from to address the needs of Asian-Americans in these churches?

Denominational structures are increasingly unreliable in a post-denominational world. Independent churches are now leading the way, and independence has strengths, but their lack of institutional structures renders interventions largely ad hoc. One phenomenon that might be noteworthy for Asian-American ecclesial life is the increasing Pentecostalization or charismati-zation of North American evangelicalism. The potential in such developments might be that the diversity and egalitarianism at the heart of the Pentecost narrative might renew and even diversify evangelical churches and leadership.[17] Yet the reality is either that most Pentecostal or charismatic churches have made little inroads into a fairly traditionalist Asian-American evangelical community or that the most vital aspects of the Pentecost vision of the church have been largely domesticated within American evangelicalism.

Transforming Evangelical Theological Education

The road to deracialization lies ahead of us. This means that we are back to the fundamental institutions that can shape such projects: educational ones. In this last part of my reflections, then, I turn to the arena I know best, the world of theological education, in which I live and work. Given space constraints, I will make only three sets of brief remarks.

First, there is no way forward except to diversity evangelical theological education. This has to do not only with the diversity of Asian-American evangelicalism,[18] but also with the diversity of worldwide evangelicalism and the fact that the center of gravity of world Christianity is increasingly shifting to the Global South. The problem, though, is that evangelicalism has understood itself largely as a theologically conservative, rather than progressive, movement. This means that the historical canon, norms, and traditions are privileged. In a global context, however, such Western and even Anglo-American perspectives may be neither as translatable nor as portable across cultures as we might think. They may not even be theologically viable. Instead, the foundations of white evangelical theology may actually inhibit the emergence of a globally relevant and engaging evangelicalism. Asian-Americans may have something to contribute to this venture, given their transnational perspectives, interests, and sensitivities. For instance, they can contribute to the articulation of a thoroughly biblical and contextual evangelical theology, even for the North American and Western world—one that appreciates, but does not impose, inappropriately classical (Western) norms, canons, and perspectives.[19]

Second, however, the diversification of evangelical theological education does not mean only the absorption of non-Western (or Asian) materials, ideas, and perspectives. Any cross-cultural encounter and dialogue ought to be a two-way street. There is much that Asian traditions—cultural, philosophical, and religious—offer for theological reflection. However, much also ought to be confronted. For instance, we must challenge Asian hierarchicalism, authoritarianism, and patriarchalism with relevant biblical norms retrieved during and since the Enlightenment.[20] These are sensitive issues that some traditionalist Asians would want to protect, even under the banner of multiculturalism or in the (supposed) "best interests of the Asian community." Yet the voices of women and of a generation of informed youth are already being heard, given the proliferation of media technologies, so we can hardly pretend that these are negligible forces and constituencies if we are working toward a post-racist evangelicalism.

Last, but not least, we have to consider strategically how to involve Asian-American perspectives in the construction of a post-racist North American evangelical culture, church, and set of institutions. Perhaps the place to begin is in our institutions of theological education. This involves not just curricular issues related to Asian-American theological writings, although that is surely important.[21] Just as important, however, are the construction, maintenance, and development of our institutions. If tokenism is to be repudiated, then how should we proceed? I suggest three lines of consideration. (1) Evangelicals should encourage and support the formation of Asian-American institutions of theological education that would focus specifically on developing Asian-American church leaders for ethnic churches. However, these should be constructed as partnerships, as much as possible. Collaboration between Asians and non-Asians will help us clarify how Asian "assimilation" can proceed without the abandonment of Asian commitments, or how non-Asian "embrace" might look that preserves the integrity of Asians and other "colored" forms of life. (2) Explicitly multicultural programs of study should be developed in predominantly white institutions of theological education. These would of course be staffed multiculturally and would seek to engage Asians, other people of color, and whites in mutual conversation and deliberation about the future of a post-racist and globally conscious North American evangelicalism. (3) Asian-American and other evangelical institutions of theological education should also forge partnerships with such institutions across the Asian world. In a time of increasing possibilities of communication, there is no reason why seminars cannot be conducted globally in which Americans (including Asian-Americans) and Asians can share ideas, address issues of common concern, and work together to shape a vibrant, global, evangelical identity. The emergence of China as a major superpower and the growing role of Asian economies in the world market suggest that the church will be increasingly marginalized if its theological educators do not awaken to the pressing needs of a globally diffused evangelicalism.

I hope it is clear that the preceding suggestions for a post-racist evangelicalism do not mean that race becomes invisible. There is now no way to get behind or even beyond race. What we all hope for is a world in which we are redeemed from racism, even as we find that the gifts of the many tongues, tribes, peoples, ethnicities, and races are celebrated as anticipations of the coming reign of God. Other Asian-American theologians and scholars have begun to reflect on these matters. Much work needs to be done. For the sake of Asian-Americans, North American evangelicals, and the worldwide church, may the conversation continue.[22]

4

Serving Alongside Latinos in a Multiethnic, Transnational, Rapidly Changing World[1]

Juan Martínez

MY LIFE IS A REFLECTION of the complexities of US Latino identity, particularly along the US-Mexico border. My mother's ancestors (Guerra) arrived in what is now South Texas when it was still a part of Spain. In five generations, they went from being Spaniards to being Mexicans (as Mexico became independent of Spain) to being US citizens (as the United States took the Southwest from Mexico). The Guerras lived and died in the same region, but they changed citizenship as outside forces determined their future. As I tell people, "My ancestors did not migrate across the border; the border migrated across my ancestors."

My father (Martínez) reflects the other side of the border experience. He was born in the Mexican border state of Nuevo León, though some of his siblings were born in the United States. Because he was one of those born in Mexico, he became an undocumented worker in Texas. There he met and married my mother. They were migrant workers during the first years of their marriage, and each one of my siblings was born in a different part of the United States.

The story is more complex because my mother's family was Protestant, ever since my great-great-grandmother had a conversion experience in South Texas. As Latino Protestants, we were part of a religious minority within an ethnic minority. After a few years of marriage, my parents heard God's call and became pastors of Latino churches in South Texas and then in Central California. That made me a fifth-generation US citizen and a fifth-generation Latino Protestant, a rare bird indeed.

Growing up as a *Protestante* meant living as a doubly marginalized person. The Catholic majority marginalized us in our Latino communities. But "Anglo" Protestants also marginalized us because we were "Mexicans."[2] It was within this community that God called me to ministry. Like my parents, and the majority of Latino pastors to this day, I attended a Latino Bible institute.[3] There I added to the complexity of my Latino identity because I met, and later married, Olga González, a Cuban-American who had grown up in Los Angeles after migrating from Cuba.

During the 1980s, Olga and I pastored Latino congregations in the racially defined environment of Central California and later in Southern California. I became a leader in my denomination, Mennonite Brethren, and found myself the token Latino on various committees and boards. Although I earned an M.Div. from the Mennonite Brethren Seminary, I could usually anticipate being talked down to because I was Latino and pastored a rural Latino church.[4] Since I had an M.Div. and spoke English, I was also asked, on more than one occasion, why I spoke Spanish and taught my children Spanish. Spanish was considered the language of poor, uneducated farm workers, something one left behind when one "got educated."

Because I became a Latino leader, I was also perceived as potentially problematic. I was called the César Chávez of the Mennonite Brethren (not meant as a compliment, coming from Central California farm owners), and eventually I was "encouraged" to leave my denominational responsibilities.

It was in this complexity that I learned several important lessons for ministry. If I was going to minister effectively as a Latino, I had to be polycentric. I had to understand and interact effectively with the various Latino communities, but I also had to understand the majority culture well if I was going to have an impact in the long term. I also learned that, though my ancestors had arrived in the Southwest in the 1700s, people whose ancestors arrived in the late 1800s (or later) would consider me a "foreigner" because their roots were in Northern Europe. I needed to make peace with the fact that I was considered a stranger, an exile, in my own land.

In 1992, we were invited to Guatemala to lead the inter-Mennonite seminary, SEMILLA. Olga and I had always wanted to spend time in Latin America, because we knew that we would better understand the immigrant segment of the US Latino community if we saw the world from a Southern perspective. Those almost nine years in Guatemala were great in many ways. But what stood out for me was that I did not have to constantly "explain" myself to people. I felt like I had come "home to a place [I'd] never been before."[5]

But I knew that my people were the "exiles" in the United States. So in 2001 I accepted the leadership of the Hispanic Center at Fuller Theological Seminary. Life at Fuller has been very enjoyable. I am involved in Latino leadership development, my vocation and passion. But preparing leaders to serve in the Latino community means addressing the complexities of Latino reality, be it history, migration, demographic changes, or the many needs within the community. We are growing in the midst of many disruptive changes, and that is creating fear and insecurity for many in the United States. People like Samuel Huntington see Latinos as a threat to US national identity.[6] Of course, I disagree. But they bring to the fore a question we must ask ourselves: "What is our vision for the future of the United States?" If Huntington's vision should be the future, then Latinos are a threat. If we can envision a different future, then Latinos, and all minority groups, are a contribution to what the United States could become.

Of course, being at Fuller also raises more mundane challenges. Most Latino Pentecostal churches question the value of seminary education, and many other Latino Protestant churches have seen how US seminaries have educated young Latinos "out" of the community. Most Latino pastors today are products of Latino Bible institutes, some of the few places where Latinos are in charge of the formation of their own leaders. Seminary education is also expensive, outside the reach of most bivocational Latino pastors. Because most Latino churches do not value seminary education, because Latino Bible institutes focus on the direct needs of Latino pastors, and because they are much cheaper, what role does Fuller play in forming Latino leaders for Latino churches?

Most Latino Protestants are Pentecostals, which means that most of the students in the Hispanic Center are already in ministry and do not need a degree from Fuller to pastor. They study at Fuller as part of their continuing education, not to be ordained. Many of these students are on the fringe of US Protestantism and do not regularly have to interact with the power structures of majority-culture churches. They study in the Hispanic Center at Fuller because they realize the importance of a formation that addresses their specific ministry realities. Because the Hispanic Center has been on the fringe of Fuller, we have been relatively free, like Latino Bible institutes, to speak directly to the issues that these pastors and leaders face.

But I also have to answer the question, "How do we move toward the center of the seminary (and of US denominations, and so on) without losing *our* center?" US seminaries want more Latino students. But do they want Latinos in leadership, guiding the direction of those seminaries? Do Protestant churches and denominations want Latino pastors and leaders? Or do they want Latinos only as long as they "look (and act) like them"?

Also, how does a US seminary prepare leaders from, and for, a community that is in the midst of significant internal and external changes—moving, adapting, and reframing a *mestizo* community in the midst of creating new *mestizajes*? The US Latino experience includes conquest, migration, assimilation, exile, opportunity, loss, adaptation, struggle, and success.[7] How do we prepare leaders for this moving target that might be 29 percent of the US population by 2050?[8]

Latinos even make life difficult for the Census Bureau—and all race-based categorizing. This is because we are not a "race," even though race continues to be one of the key categories for defining the US experience. The category "Latino" defies most attempts to define us because we are so diverse. We have many national, linguistic, ethnic, and racial backgrounds. And as we continue to grow in the United States, more people will speak Spanish, even as more Latinos become English-dominant or monolingual speakers. We will intermarry, though often into other minority groups (particularly African-American), not necessarily assimilating into the majority. Because of the various ways in which we have become a part of the United States, including us in the US narrative will be difficult and painful, because, once again, the United States will have to deal with its history of conquest and empire. We are part of the harvest of the US imperial expansion.[9]

Serving Latinos in a US Seminary Environment

Latinos remind US seminaries that effective seminary education needs to address a broad range of issues and their impact on church and mission, be it culture and language, ethnic identity, migration, interethnic relations, or transnationalism. It also has to address the existential fear faced by many in the "Christian" West because the growing edge of the church is now in the South. The West may have the money and the institutions, but the rest of the world is going forward with or without the support of Western Christians. Will the expansion of the church in the South be seen as something to fear or as an opportunity to join in what God is doing in the world? Effective seminary education means helping students recognize that all areas of theological education, be it theology, Bible, history, or ministry, are affected by these issues.

I want to address two aspects of the task. On the one hand, I want to mention ways in which US seminaries can serve Latino leaders more effectively. But I also want to invite seminaries to think about how to prepare pastors and leaders for the more diverse world reflected by the growth of Latinos and other minority communities.

Moving Forward: Preparing Latinos for Service in the Latino Community in US Seminaries

Because of the diversity of the Latino community, it is impossible to describe one plan that would effectively prepare all Latinos for all the types of ministry in which Latinos participate. So I want to focus on the formation of Latinos who are working or are preparing to work predominantly in the Latino community.

Seminaries, denominations, and missionaries have struggled with how to prepare pastors effectively for ministry in Latino churches ever since the first Latino congregations were formed in the Southwest in the 1850s. Bible institutes and informal preparation became the standard, though the first formal seminary-type program was started in the 1890s by Presbyterians in southern Colorado.[10]

The Bible institute became the principal means of theological formation for most Latino pastors, particularly those from Pentecostal denominations, those whose principal language was Spanish, or those who had limited formal education. US seminaries have always had a small number of Latino students, though many of them have come from Latin America. But seminaries have not always been Latino-friendly. They have usually been out of the reach of most US Latinos, mostly because of their educational requirements, cost, or linguistic limitations. The small numbers that have attended seminary have often found that they received a solid biblical, theological, and historical formation, but few tools for connecting that knowledge to the reality of their ministry. And Latino churches that sent their young people to seminary were often frustrated because many of those young people were seemingly "educated out" of the Latino community.[11]

Latino Protestant churches are growing rapidly in the United States and currently constitute about 20 percent of the Latino population.[12] But most of the growth is happening in denominations and churches that do not require seminary education for ministry or ordination. Many churches not only do not require a seminary education of their pastors, but even question the usefulness of seminary. Yet the number of Latinos going to seminary, or wanting to go to seminary, is growing. Because seminary is not an ordination requirement for most Latino pastors and leaders, they will go to seminary for other reasons, most often as a form of continuing education.

Since most Latino Protestant pastors have studied in nonaccredited Bible institutes, or in Spanish, they create a dilemma for seminaries. This dilemma is compounded by the fact that many Latinos do not have the resources to finance a seminary education easily. Many seminaries feel that they cannot respond to students with these problems. Others are ready to work with them, but often begin from assumptions of deficiency. Because these students have not followed the common educational route, seminaries develop noncredit certificates or some type of remedial program, so that they can learn master's-level English or complete a B.A. Others simply offer Latino seminarians noncredit certificate programs. The Association of Theological Schools (ATS) has provided seminaries with another option through the "10 percent rule," which allows member schools to accept up to 10 percent of their students without a B.A.[13] But some seminaries believe they should not use this option, assuming that an accredited B.A. is indispensible in leadership development for ministry.

If seminaries want to have an impact among Latino churches, they will have to decide if and how they will work alongside Bible institutes. Many of them have very solid programs, but accreditation is rarely a realistic option for them. Bible institutes are also among the few educational institutions where Latinos are in charge. They have the flexibility to accept most Latino leaders and are usually very inexpensive. Since the majority of Latino pastors are being trained in Bible institutes, seminaries can provide curricular support, training of professors and administrators, and other support that strengthens these programs. This gives seminaries a much broader impact and also helps them develop strong bridges for Bible institute graduates who want to go on to seminary.

Seminaries can also provide focused master's programs for experienced Latino pastors. This will mean that seminaries have to validate Bible institute programs. Students who are without an accredited degree, but who have extensive experience, can benefit from developing ministry portfolios, in which they describe and reflect on their ministry experiences and demonstrate that they are capable of studying at seminary. This meets the ATS 10 percent rule and also gives seminaries assurance that these students are ready for seminary-level education.

Getting Latino students to seminary is only part of the challenge. The financial reality of many of the potential students means that they will need scholarships and that they will be part-time students. Most will continue their ministries or other job commitments or both. This means that seminaries will need to have programs geared to commuting, part-time students.

But it also means asking questions about pedagogy. A theory-to-practice model will not work nearly as well as a praxis model that draws on the experiences of these pastors to help them connect new learning to their ministries. This model will also make it easier for Latinos to make the connections between what they are learning in seminary and the complexities of the environment in which they minister.

Latino students are also crucial for seminaries. Many of them bring a transnational experience, a cultural, social, and linguistic diversity, and a different experience of Christian faith—all of which create challenges for seminaries, but which are also indispensible assets. A large percentage of Latino churches in the United States reflect the dynamic spirituality of the majority world, a spirituality more attuned to the working of the Spirit in the world today and one that may be better able to respond to postmodern reality. This means that seminaries also need to develop ways for non-Latinos to learn from their Latino colleagues about life and ministry in an increasingly diverse world.

Seminary programs will best be able to serve Latino students when they include:

- Latino faculty with ministry experience among US Latinos. Students need mentors and models, not only professors. A praxis model of education will also be strengthened when professors are able to draw from their own ministry and life experiences.

- Language-flexible programs. Most immigrant pastors work most comfortably in Spanish. Many US-born and US-educated pastors minister in Spanish much of the time or in both English and Spanish. Programs that recognize and support this reality are most able to provide a learning environment conducive to ministry preparation.

- Courses that address the complexities of ministry in the Latino community, but also deal with the increasingly multicultural environment of ministry in the United States.

- Courses that allow and expect students to "read the Bible in Spanish"[14] and to reflect theologically from their own experience and that of their parishioners.

- Cohorts, mentors, and various support systems, so that students have a strong, high-touch support base for part-time studies.

- Field education programs that value Latino churches and connect non-Latino students to these churches as places of learning for all.

- Programs that work alongside Latino churches to identify and support a new generation of Latino pastors who can become fully bilingual and multicultural, if given support and encouragement.

Seminary impact in the Latino community will depend on seminaries rethinking some of their ministry assumptions, their teaching models, and their understanding of their role in society. It will also mean recognizing that Latinos and other minority groups are changing and enriching the United States. This means that seminaries need to make changes to prepare Latino leaders effectively, but it also means that they have to think differently about how to prepare non-Latinos to serve in this changing environment.

Preparing Non-Latinos to Serve among Latinos and Other Minority Peoples

President Richard Mouw of Fuller Seminary recently asked several minority faculty members to read and analyze our "Mission beyond the Mission" statement in light of the changes taking place at the beginning of the twenty-first century.[15] In my response, I both affirmed what had been done in the past and called the seminary to a different future. My colleague, Jehu Hanciles,[16] and I addressed many important issues, some of which are beyond the scope of this article. But we also addressed issues like migration, transnationalism, and Southern Christianity. These are issues that seminaries, denominations, and churches cannot ignore if Latinos and other minority and immigrant groups are going to "fit" (i.e., be accepted) in the broader US church. Are US majority-culture Christians ready to address a world where they are not the majority and where the most dynamic parts of the church are Southern based or Southern oriented? Are US seminaries, denominations, and churches willing to prepare leaders for a world where migration continues to change the role of the nation-state and to redefine ethnic and national identities?

Western Christians have often assumed that crossing cultural and ethnic boundaries with the gospel is something that is done "over there" wherever "mission" is being done. The church has been much less successful at intercultural or interethnic ministry. Yet that is one of the underlying narratives in the book of Acts and one of the key issues we need to address as we prepare leaders to minister in the twenty-first-century United States.

During my years at Fuller, I have worked closely with my colleague, Mark Lau Branson. We have taught courses together in English and Spanish at both the master's and the doctoral level (D.Min.). The focus of our teaching, and also a book, has been on working and leading in this changing, multicultural environment.[17] We have drawn from our experiences as pastors, from our research, and from the experiences of our students, many of whom are struggling together through these issues.

Probably the most important lesson we teach our students is that this is plain hard work. Popular multiculturalism draws on the surface products of culture (music, food, dress, sometimes even language) and assumes that if these are present we have effectively drawn people together. Learning to interact with the cultural productions of others is important, but it is merely the starting point, not the goal. There will be much harder questions to address, once we start down this path, such as:

- What is our vision of God's future? How do we envision the Revelation 7:9–10 worship scene? How does that vision impact how we do church today?

- What is our political vision of the United States? How is it impacted by our vision of the kingdom? And which informs which? My experience is that our political vision often colors our vision of the kingdom, much more than the other way around.

- Over the last five centuries, church and mission have often been tied to political and colonial power. Are we ready to break those molds?

- How do we deal with the sense of displacement that many majority-culture Christians will feel as minority groups become the majority in the United States?

- How do we break the patterns of racial identity politics that see others, particularly those from ethnic minority groups, as the "problem"?

Elizabeth Conde-Frazier has written an excellent article in which she describes the process by which we can move toward a kingdom vision of interethnic relations in the United States (and beyond). In "From Hospitality to Shalom," she describes an important, but difficult and complex process of moving from "making room" for each other to actually working together toward a common goal, God's *shalom*. The article takes us from *hospitality*, which opens us up, to the possibility of an *encounter*, where we get to know each other, but also confront the realities of our differences and our very real tensions. As we learn about the depths of each other's particular experiences and why these are important, we can feel real *compassion* for the other. From compassion comes the willingness to walk alongside the other, from which can come a *passion* for the issues that are important to them. Once there, we can approach *shalom*, that place where we minister together as equals and from where we see real hope for reconciliation. It is here that we begin to be willing to distribute power equally and become ready to live on the margin with the marginalized, for the sake of the gospel.[18]

What Conde-Frazier proposes is no easy task. Yet, if the church is to respond to the increasingly multiethnic world in which we live, then we need leaders to embody and lead churches in the journey from hospitality to shalom. This process has to affect everything from our theology to our reading of Scripture, including how we approach ministry. But this is principally about who we are as people before God and how we understand our role as leaders in God's work in the world.

Addressing what Conde-Frazier proposes has important implications for US seminary education. Seminaries cannot create the conversion, but they can create opportunities for the process to begin. Most seminary students will not easily move toward shalom unless it is a planned part of their seminary education. Many seminaries provide opportunities for hospitality across ethnic and cultural lines, but it is usually with the "other" who is "over there" or with the few nonwhite seminarians, who often feel like tokens in this process.[19] Nonetheless, we need to strengthen those hospitality opportunities, so that we can create the space for encounter.

Encounter happens when we immerse ourselves in the experiences of the other. We do it in class by inviting all students to share their cultural and religious narratives and by having them interact with the experiences of those with whom they might otherwise have little interaction. Seminaries can expand these opportunities by requiring students to participate in ministry settings outside their cultural comfort zones. Taking the time to understand my own cultural framing and its impact on my life makes it possible for me to value the experiences of the other. This breaks me out of stereotypes, allowing me to humanize the other and begin the process of encounter.

True encounter forces me to confront my interpretations of reality. Some of us want to practice compassion without encounter. But that type of compassion makes the other the object of my mission, based on my understanding their needs. Encounter faces me with the fact that all of us have incomplete understandings of our world. Compassion based on encounter listens to the other before offering responses. This type of compassion can lead to passion and beyond.

But one obvious barrier to encounter is the unwillingness to confront our perceptions of reality. Majority culture (conservative or liberal) tends to have a narrative of the "exceptional" status of the United States. This view puts Anglo America at the center of "God's plan" (conservative) or of "human destiny" (liberal) and interprets others in the light of this understanding. Others (nonwhites) have a place to the extent that they "become like us." Huntington was correct in assuming that Latinos, like other minority groups, are a threat to that understanding of the United States and of what God is doing in the world. But God's work in the world is much bigger than the vision of one country, even the United States.

The move from compassion to passion and then to shalom is the work of the Holy Spirit. But if seminaries provide the opportunities for hospitality and encounter, then the next generation of leaders can continue growing toward shalom. One of the roles of leadership is to interpret reality. Therefore, we need leaders in the process of moving "from hospitality to shalom" to help the church in the United States understand and join in what God is doing in the world. Seminaries can help US pastors and leaders envision a different future by creating opportunities for encounter in the classroom, in seminary life, and in field education. But trustees, senior administration, faculty, and staff also need to model this process in seminaries as a whole. As "hospitality to shalom" informs how seminaries relate to Latinos and other ethnic minorities, they will be able to form leaders who are able to move toward compassion, passion, and shalom.

Latino Christians are part of the vision of God's future, and they will be a growing part of the United States in the years to come. As we grow, we will also become more diverse. How Latino and majority-culture Christians interact will be strongly influenced by our visions of God's future. That is why it is crucial to reflect on biblical visions of the future. Will the kingdom take first place in defining our future, or will our national and political perspectives? The challenges raised by the Latino community will grow in increasing complexity. Our faithfulness to God's mission will depend on our willingness to struggle through these issues in light of God's future.

> After this I looked, and there was a great multitude that no one could count, from every nation, from all tribes and peoples and languages, standing before the throne and before the Lamb, robed in white, with palm branches in their hands. They cried out in a loud voice, saying,
>
> "Salvation belongs to our God who is seated on the throne, and to the Lamb!" (Rev. 7:9–10 NRSV)

73

5

ETHNIC SCARCITY IN EVANGELICAL THEOLOGY: WHERE ARE THE AUTHORS?

Vincent Bacote

IN SOME WAYS, this chapter revisits and updates my very first journal article,[1] though with a more specific focus on the relatively small number of African-American and Latino scholars of theological and biblical studies. Following an introductory section that portrays the conservative Protestant landscape through a biographical lens, I will offer three suggestions for moving toward a more diverse composition of scholars in conservative Protestant institutions.

Although I regard myself as somewhat culturally fluid, the realities of race in the United States are inescapable. I am the second oldest in my family; my older brother was born in 1963, and I followed eighteen months later in 1965. In that time, the Civil Rights Act of 1964 was signed into law, outlawing many forms of racial discrimination and removing obstacles for African-American voter registration. One of my earliest memories comes from 1968, when my uncle took me, along with my mother and two brothers, to a nearby railway where the train carrying Robert F. Kennedy's casket went by. While I remember a train going by, I had no sense of its significance, though I later recall my mother recounting that my uncle cried as the train sped past.

The majority of my childhood took place during the 1970s, and my formative Christian experience came primarily through attending Shiloh Baptist Church in Glenarden, Maryland. While it is a member church of both the National and the Progressive Baptist Conventions, the ethos of the church was rarely, or ever, political. Seldom was there conversation about whether our church should be integrated or about specific political concerns, yet I became aware that there were some religious people who believed that the races should remain separate. My earliest memories related to race relations stem from my curiosity about what "black" and "white" meant, from listening to conversations between relatives, and from media portrayals of race relations. Among the first controversies were the integration of public schools and the Bob Jones court case related to interracial dating. I experienced the latter, and, contrary to my fears and nervous expectations, it was a very positive experience that actually facilitated my own cultural hybridization. Unlike my parents, I had both white and black friends. I had no negative experiences related to race, and, in a way, I became a "child of integration," who for a time thought the solution to racism was the embrace of color-blindness.

While I grew up in a confessionally orthodox context, I had little idea of what evangelicalism was until I went to college at The Citadel, the military college in South Carolina. I was significantly shaped by my participation in the Navigators, a parachurch organization. I learned a lot about the Bible and

Christian discipleship. The word *evangelical* was not a term we used, but it was during this period that I was first exposed to popular evangelical figures like Chuck Swindoll. I also encountered my first tension between Christianity and race during the 1984 presidential election. Having grown up in a home where no one ever suggested that voting Republican was a live option, I was shocked to encounter friends in my Bible study who thought only of voting Republican (in fact, it seemed that the majority of my classmates were Republicans). This did not cause any difficulties in my friendships, because I rarely discussed politics. But I was perplexed, because I had little understanding of the tainted racial histories of both parties. For example, I was unaware that it was a relatively new, post-1964 allegiance that African-Americans had to the Democrats. As one born on the other side of the shift, it was all I knew. My own political allegiance changed as a result of my exposure to evangelical media in the years immediately after college, when I moved to Memphis, Tennessee, to volunteer with a Navigators ministry. I soon became a regular listener to Christian radio, which featured the likes of James Dobson, John MacArthur, and Charles Stanley. There were also programs that addressed the issues of the day, both cultural and political. Through this influence, along with my belief that the resolution to racial issues was to look beyond race rather than through it, I concluded that a biblically faithful approach to political issues was more in line with the Republicans than the Democrats, particularly due to issues like abortion. At the time, I felt little tension between the arguments made on Christian radio and "typical" concerns of African-Americans. Tension was apparent in the ministry context, however.

Soon after my arrival in Memphis, I learned that the campus ministry had decided to transition from a single group to two separate groups, an African-American group and a Caucasian group. This was less because of racial discord than pragmatic concerns related to how the ministry would navigate cultural differences. The two groups would come together for large events, but the Bible studies and weekly group meetings were separate. This was a strategic decision that helped the ministry grow, because it provided space for diversity in gospel communication and worship. During my time there, the entire ministry went on a ski trip to Colorado, which I thought was very enjoyable, but this was not an opinion shared by all. After I returned, I learned that some of the African-American members of the ministry found some things to be offensive: jokes made by one of the hosts, and the competitive approach on the slopes. Looking back, I believe this was actually the result of miscommunication and differences in relational styles. I was beginning to learn that even though people from different ethnic backgrounds can study the same Bible and share the same deep commitment to Christ, this does not automatically equate to identical strategies or priorities in ministry—or even mutual understanding.

I went from Memphis to Trinity Evangelical Divinity School in 1990. Before leaving Memphis, I saw that minorities had a complicated relationship with evangelicalism. I observed this primarily in parachurch organizations like the Navigators and Campus Crusade for Christ. I sensed the challenges for minorities even more clearly when I arrived at Trinity. When I arrived there, I thought that evangelical seminaries were places that could build the biblical and theological foundation of African-American churches. I mostly saw this as an issue of access to the right kind of information; I thought the key to greater biblical fidelity and more fruitful ministry was to learn what was on offer in evangelical institutions. It was unclear to me why these schools had such small minority enrollments. While cost was an issue for some, the larger issue was that these institutions were not prominently visible on the horizon of African-Americans who pursued theological education. More importantly, for many who did attend these institutions, there was what I now recognize as a cultural disconnect, particularly for those who did not have much or any familiarity with evangelicalism. To put it differently, the issue had as much to do with culture as it did with getting the right information, and I soon learned that even the latter idea was contested. My curiosity about this led me to begin research for "When Will There Be Room in the Inn?"

In 1993, I attended a conference at Geneva College in honor of Bill Bentley, who had passed away shortly before the event. The conference was meant to reflect upon African-American evangelicalism. It included Tom Skinner, William Pannell, Tony Evans, Eugene Rivers, Kenneth Kantzer, Carl F. H. Henry, and J. Deotis Roberts among the speakers. What became clear to me during the conference was that certain older African-Americans who had been part of the evangelical context were very frustrated with an evangelicalism that was focused on right belief, but which did not give much or any attention to how that faith could help the challenges in African-American communities.[2] While no one made accusations of gnosticism at the conference, the frustration could be regarded as such: a central complaint was that evangelical theology failed to take into account the concrete experiences and concerns of African-Americans.[3] More precisely, one could say that a consistent critique was that evangelical theology emphasized orthodox beliefs, but did not lead to ethical emphases that resonated with the African-American community.

I left the conference aware that evangelicalism had considerable work to do to make significant inroads into minority communities. There was a much greater disconnect than I had thought, and it was far from clear that there was much desire among African-American evangelicals to invest their time and energy in the broader evangelical world. In view of this situation, it is not at all surprising that there are so few minority authors writing on biblical and theological topics. Two specific examples may help to illuminate this further.

First, the annual meetings of the Evangelical Theological Society (ETS) are a prime example of the dearth of minority scholars and authors. While the same could be said about many academic guilds, the context in question is evangelicalism and conservative theological communities. The Evangelical Theological Society's statement of purpose declares: "The purpose of the Society shall be to foster conservative biblical scholarship by providing a medium for the oral exchange and written expression of thought and research in the general field of the theological disciplines as centered in the Scriptures."[4]

The ETS emerged in 1949 and has served as a counterpart to guilds like the Society of Biblical Literature and the American Academy of Religion. One way to think of the ETS is as an organization that has placed significant emphasis on defending conservative Christianity, particularly in response to the assumptions of modern approaches to the Bible, theology, and religion. The ETS proceeds from the conviction that the Bible is completely authoritative and trustworthy, and its scholarly conversation is focused on questions related to the integrity of the text. The emphasis is stronger on biblical studies than on theology—which should not be a surprise, because the purpose statement emphasizes "biblical scholarship" and highlights the centrality of the biblical text in other theological disciplines. The ETS is also a context where scholarly conversation is focused on prominent points of biblical/theological tension in the evangelical world, such as the proper place of ethnic Israel, the proper approach to exegesis, and eschatology.

The ETS emerged fifteen years before the Civil Rights Act of 1964, and while there certainly have been African-Americans and other nonwhite minorities who have interacted with the various communities under the umbrella of evangelicalism—

even before the twentieth century—there have been few who have published in this setting or attended the ETS annual meetings before or since that time. While there are some African-American seminary students and professors who have attended in recent decades, this is a very small number, and an even smaller number have actually presented papers.[5]

Why is this the case in a guild where the Bible is held up as God's inerrant word? Perhaps it is for the same reasons that there are few minorities in organizations across the broader evangelical landscape. Some of this is because most African-American Christians find their "home" primarily in traditional denominations, and they have had minimal or tangential exposure to guilds such as the ETS, even if they have greater awareness of them now than in prior decades. In addition, while there has been some increase in the number of minorities with doctoral degrees in biblical and theological studies, this is a small number overall, and even smaller when one considers the number of those who would embrace the purpose and doctrinal stance of the ETS. The dearth of doctoral students is a problem, not only because of minimal participation in the conservative theological world, but also because, in contexts like the African-American church, generally speaking, those interested in biblical and theological matters are directed toward the pastorate rather than the guild. In addition, the 1993 conference at Geneva College revealed that some of those who have participated in the world of conservative Protestantism have found it exasperating. With such minimal participation, any encouragement to publish, even if well intentioned, finds few ears hearing the message.

A second example is provided by evangelical publishers. In 1999, I was part of a group of African-American ministry leaders and scholars whom InterVarsity Press invited to its headquarters in an effort to create an opportunity for more writing. The group included pastors, parachurch leaders, and a small group of scholars, and the specific aim of the event was to facilitate the writing process and produce actual published work. I was a participant in the scholars' group, and we all brought draft proposals and discussed a range of book ideas. Since that event, which was a positive experience for all involved (from my recollection), there have not been many actual books produced, particularly in the scholarly trajectory. Beyond InterVarsity Press, publishers like Baker Academic, Eerdmans, and Zondervan all want book proposals from minority scholars, but the population of minority professors is small—a survey of seminaries and Christian colleges will demonstrate this fact—and their overall productivity, in terms of monographs at least, has not been very high—though one can speculate that perhaps the percentage of minority scholars with monographs is similar to that of majority scholars. Even though publishers may want to solicit books from minority scholars, the small population makes it difficult to yield many publications.

Moving Forward

What to do? How is it possible to begin to remedy this? I offer three suggestions that may begin to address this.

First, it is important for conservative Protestants to live up to their biblical ideals. For example, evangelicals are known for their commitment to the entirety of biblical truth, yet in practice this has not always been the case. As Ed Gilbreath's *Reconciliation Blues* reveals, many minorities who encounter evangelical institutions discover that they are welcome, but not without a price.[6] While these institutions want to be faithful to the entire Bible, in many cases minorities find them to be less than fully supportive. In terms of producing minority authors, it will require a greater commitment to following the second greatest commandment: "Love your neighbor as yourself" (Matt. 22:38–39; cf. Rom. 15:9). All God's laws governing our interactions are expressions of his command that we treat each other in the way we would like others to treat us. It will be impossible to produce a generation of minority theological and biblical scholars if evangelical institutions are not environments in which bright minority students discover a commitment to their flourishing, expressed not only in personal piety and academic preparation, but also in concrete efforts to understand and address the unique challenges such students face in the world of conservative Protestants.[7] This also extends to the support these scholars will need when they begin to navigate the processes of tenure and promotion once they become faculty members.

A second suggestion flows from the first: one way to begin cultivating scholarly publishing by minority students and faculty is to establish networks that would create a pipeline to evangelical institutions and publishers. As noted above, many minorities are unfamiliar with the scholarly world or even the possibility of pursuing a scholarly vocation in contrast or addition to pastoral ministry. Initiative from all communities is necessary, but it is particularly important for conservative Protestant institutions to continue working to recruit students to colleges and seminaries, and for members of the faculty and administration to identify, mentor, and encourage those students for whom the scholarly vocation may be ideal. To develop such networks, conservative Protestant institutions need to establish relationships with historically minority denominations (e.g., National Baptist, African Methodist Episcopal, Church of God in Christ) and cultivate trust, so that leadership and congregants may direct bright students to colleges and seminaries (and ultimately to doctoral programs). While not an easy task, this is a necessity if there is to be a larger group of minority scholars who identify as conservative Protestants and who will also write scholarly articles and monographs.

The third suggestion is vital for establishing the trust necessary for networks and a pipeline: take seriously the theological questions that are central to minorities. One reason there are few minority scholars at meetings like those of the Evangelical Theological Society is that when such scholars *have* come, they have found the conversation peripheral to their concerns and have found the ethos dissonant with their important questions of method, doctrine, and interpretation. This is not to suggest that liberation theology must be a central focus, but rather that it is extremely important to create an ethos where one considers how fidelity to the Bible interacts with the questions of individual and social experience that are unavoidable to minorities. One way to think of this is that the bifurcation between theology and ethics is untenable for those who come from communities where the confession and practice of faith are inextricably linked, thus making matters of faith also matters of politics, culture, and psychology. As an example, conversations about a theological response to the problem of evil might need to focus on the history of lynching in the United States or on narratives about the travails of immigrants from Latin America. If the conversation in these circles extends *beyond* traditional conservative Protestant emphases (this involves expanding the conversation, not replacing it), then an ethos will exist that may catalyze the work of minority scholars.

To conclude: in the years since I wrote my first article, I have seen some changes, but there is a long path ahead. I hope that more minority scholars will emerge and form a generation of authors who will make a much needed contribution to the academy and the church, but I know that a long gestation will probably be required. I hope that birth will come, by God's grace, and that we will give glory to God for the fruit that springs from future generations.

6

BLACKS AND LATINOS IN THEOLOGICAL EDUCATION AS PROFESSORS AND ADMINISTRATORS

Harold Dean Trulear

THREE FUNDAMENTAL (pun intended) observations frame this essay. First, I believe that the history of American evangelicalism reveals it to be a fundamentally (okay, no more puns) reactionary movement, from the fundamentalist reaction to modernism to the neo-evangelical reaction to the stridency of fundamentalism in the 1950s. As such, the movement has grown accustomed to living in a reactionary tone, which reveals an inherent battle with defenses.

Second, revisionist history to the contrary,[1] American evangelicalism persists as a movement based on rational assent to propositional orthodoxy, especially in its educational and other institutional forms. Attempts to include the heroic efforts of black denominations and the ministry of Martin Luther King Jr. simply require a broadening of the evangelical DNA of propositional orthodoxy, which previously excluded those persons and churches from the movement. Although I reject the characterization of African-American Christianity as "fallen," as proffered by black Reformed thinker Thabiti Anyabwile,[2] I do not accept that the historic notion of evangelicalism ought to be broadened to include traditions and ministries that do not hold to propositional orthodoxy as the badge of fidelity. On a personal note, the older I become, the more Calvinism appeals to me, but the fact that the majority of my colleagues offering essays in this volume represent strong Reformed traditions bids me to rebut them on this point.

Third, as a sociologist, I must distinguish between race and ethnicity for the purposes of this discussion. Race is a political and social fact; ethnicity is a cultural one. As a political fact, race refers to meaning and convention assigned to individuals based on appearance, i.e., color of skin, facial features, hair texture, and so on. Ethnicity refers to the cultural heritage of a given social group, bound by meanings developed in particular social contexts. Put simply, *black* and *Latino/a* are racial designations, while *African-American*, *Mexican-American*, *Puerto Rican*, and so on are ethnic designations. When we encounter a black person, he or she could be from any of a variety of ethnic groups with different culturally based meaning systems and interpretations, none of which matter when they are pulled over by the police for DWB (Driving While Black) or are subject to other forms of racial profiling. That a Latina woman hails from Puerto Rico and not Cuba matters greatly to her understanding of ethnic dialogue, especially when a denomination sends a Colombian woman to pastor a congregation of Dominicans on the assumption that "they are all Latinos." Therefore, I will use the terms *black* and *Latino/a* specifically to refer to race, and *African-American, Chicano, Jamaican, Haitian, Dominican,* and so on to refer specifically to ethnic groups with distinctive, albeit sometimes related or overlapping, meaning systems and cultures. In several cases below, confusion over race and ethnicity has presented both challenge and opportunity to evangelical institutions.

These three assertions frame my remarks because they at once reflect issues in my personal experience during my journey to and through evangelicalism, and because, as a seminary professor and administrator for over three decades, I know that institutions matter, and their inherently conservative (sociologically, not theologically) nature tends to reify definitions in ways that mitigate against change. Therefore, they frame the first section of the essay, in which I relate how I discovered my evangelicalism and began to work in and with evangelical institutions. The three assertions provide context for the second section of the essay because any challenges to existing institutional convention must reflect precision in definition when confronting the *realpolitik* of institutional inertia.

What I have tried to do below is to relate my personal story while interacting with the significant literature and research on blacks and American evangelical higher education.[3] The latter body of work concentrates almost exclusively on undergraduate education, save when a seminary exists as part of a Christian university. So we still await definitive work on race and American evangelical seminaries. In the end, I find hope in the movement from the ignorance and hostility I experienced in the early 1970s, when I discovered that I was an evangelical, to the current state of affairs, where the black and Latino presence has grown to the point where the discussion of a multicultural vision for American evangelical education flows from its existential reality, and not just from theory.

Somewhere to Lay My Head[4]

My journey to evangelicalism reads more like an example of Calvinist predestination than the result of a conscious decision to embrace the movement. I was raised in a high-church, middle-class, African-American, Episcopalian congregation with a storied history of political activism. I first heard liberation theology, not in a seminary classroom, but from the pulpit. The preaching came from our youth minister—one of the cofounders of the Institute for Black Ministries, a liberation theology think tank located in the former Conwell School of Theology building at Temple University. Although formed liturgically and ecclesiastically by the congregation, my spiritual growth came from several evangelical sources. First, I confessed Christ as my Savior at a Bible Club Ministries camp—Camp Streamside—as a nine-year-old in 1964. Second, my best friend from childhood, Gregory Palmer, now a United Methodist bishop, served as a "spiritual director" through my adolescence. Additionally, I played in several classical music groups with an evangelical family, the Matthews, one of whose number—Professor Ronald Matthews—currently serves as professor of music at Eastern University. At the time, I did not know they were "evangelicals"; in fact, I had never heard the term. Rather, they just seemed like "Christians" to me, and my youth minister seemed somewhere between weird and heretical.

The term *evangelical* came to me when I became a volunteer for Youth for Christ and Campus Life while a student at Morehouse College in 1973. The staff there was looking for a musician to become part of its music ministry team, and it especially wanted an African-American musician who could also serve as a volunteer in one of its new Campus Life clubs, ministering at a predominantly African-American high school. I was recruited from the Morehouse music department, went through volunteer training, was handed a book by Tom

Skinner, and thus became officially enrolled in the American evangelical movement.

The training had no cultural sensitivity to it, and I am not talking about being sensitive to how to reach African-American students—I mean no cultural sensitivity whatsoever. My first staff team included a gentleman who "didn't like blacks, until I met you." Our training sessions included an admonition to follow Paul's challenge to be "content in whatsoever state" we find ourselves, with the slaves in *Gone with the Wind* as a contemporary example. "They was singing like birds," our trainer proffered, as a challenge to comply with the Pauline injunction. Evangelicalism was beginning to scare me.

The redemption of the term came when InterVarsity Christian Fellowship appeared on the Morehouse campus during my junior year. Staff member Tony Warner, so revered now in his fifth decade of black campus ministry that we call him "the Bishop," discipled me through my reluctance to identify with such a racially charged interpretation of the movement, and prayed with and for me when a sister staff member told me that interracial marriage was against God's will.

I had no trouble signing on to Youth for Christ's doctrinal statement. I did struggle with what I saw as a reactionary posture against those who were deemed "liberal." Though I had similar disagreements with my church as a teenager, I did not approach the difference with such stridency. I concluded that evangelicals, at least the white ones, were more concerned about doctrine than people, and, had it not been for brother Warner and IVCF, I would have declared myself not to be "one of those." When I moved my YFC staff position to North Jersey, I found less stridency, but still more "fidelity to doctrine" language than that to which I was accustomed. Loving Christian relationships and concern for the poor, justice, and so on did not appear on the radar screen. One veteran staff member even confided to me that had we been with YFC during the period of American slavery, he would have supported it as a biblical institution.

InterVarsity became my evangelical haven, in large measure because of its willingness to struggle with the deep issues of race and ethnicity, class and justice. The race and ethnicity issue loomed large because of the large numbers of black students of Caribbean descent who, though black, had a different culture and view of race relations from black students from the United States. InterVarsity's willingness to institutionalize the struggle by creating the office of Multiethnic Ministries, with a vice president overseeing its work, cemented it as an evangelical movement light years ahead of the reactionary doctrinal battles fought elsewhere. Likewise, it fostered credible dialogue between proponents and opponents of such a distinct department within its ranks.

InterVarsity struggled nobly with the tension within the black student community, often between younger black students—especially second-generation African and Caribbean students in the United States—and the older African-Americans for whom the race issue continued to loom large because of the injustices of the pre-1980s era within the United States in general and American evangelicalism in particular. IVCF's willingness to take its global missions work, notably its Urbana missions conference, and read back through it into the various trajectories represented among people of color, enabled it to create a context for dialogue that continues today. IVCF, unlike much of American evangelicalism, recognized not only the distinctive reality of African-Americans participating in the movement, but also the cultural distinction within the black student population it served. My service as a speaker, volunteer, and board member represented one of two high points of participating in the movement.

The other high point was my involvement with the Center for Urban Theological Studies (CUTS) in Philadelphia. Curiously (providentially?), it sprang from the same vacuum that created the Institute for Black Ministries—the departure of the Conwell School of Theology at Temple University to Boston to merge with Gordon Divinity School in 1970. CUTS developed in the educational vacuum created by that departure in a manner that reflected the African-American community's rejection of the more radical forms of liberation theology taught at the Institute. Originally organized by Westminster Theological Seminary and their alum Bill Krispin, CUTS has labored long and hard to develop racial and cultural sensitivity—including providing a supportive educational environment for female African-American clergy, which Westminster, by mission and denominational connection, cannot do.

CUTS provides undergraduate and graduate ministerial education for second-career African-American adults through evening classes leading toward associate's, bachelor's, and master's degrees, which are granted by Lancaster Bible College. I taught at CUTS from 1987 through 2003, and also served on its board in the mid-1990s, and was vice chair of the search committee that brought the first African-American president—Verley Sangster—to CUTS.

In its early years, CUTS reflected much of the doctrinaire reactionary posture mentioned above. The presence was subtle, but one could hear it in classrooms where women were not permitted to lead the class in prayer, and one could see it in the composition of the faculty. Through the late 1980s, for example, virtually all the "academic" courses—Bible, theology, ethics, church history—were taught by white faculty. Black faculty— African-Americans like me and Caribbean-Americans like Wesley Pinnock—were confined to "ministry" courses. I finally went to the dean and offered that CUTS could allow me, as a

Ph.D. who had taught ethics and earned tenure at an accredited seminary, to teach more than "Youth Ministry." When in 1989 I taught Introduction to Christian Ethics, I was the only African-American instructor in an academic course. This has changed drastically over the past twenty years, and CUTS's tradition of placing justice and relationships at the center of its mission, initially in the form of commitment to racial reconciliation, created space for a healthy, if uneven, growth in becoming a comfortable place for African-Americans in preparation for ministry.

My time at CUTS brought me into conversation with a number of faculty and administrators of Christian colleges and universities across the country. Both major associations of Christian Colleges—the Christian College Consortium and the Coalition of Christian Colleges and Universities—entered the nascent stage of engaging a multiplicity of ethnic traditions at the levels of student population, faculty, administration, and governance. A few years as a travelling multiculturalism consultant for these schools in the early 1990s opened my eyes to the good intentions of some, the recalcitrance of others, and the cluelessness of yet a third group. As Theodore Cross and Robert Bruce Slater have documented, much has changed for the better.[5] Yet challenges remain. The remaining portion of this essay is my attempt to list these challenges, based on observation and research, experience and reading.

Moving Forward: Challenges for Evangelical Institutions of Higher Education

Geography and Demographics

Theology and mission notwithstanding, Christian higher education faces challenges that have less to do with mission and more to do with the state of higher education in America. Evangelical colleges, universities, and seminaries reflect geographical and demographic realities that challenge many institutions of higher learning. When evangelical institutions are compared with nonsectarian peer institutions, the number of African-American faculty, staff, and students do not differ dramatically. Liberal arts colleges in remote rural areas of the Midwest do not draw significant numbers of black and African-American students. Outside of athletics, where the number of blacks participating in prestigious and revenue-generating sports such as basketball and football is high, there is little to draw an urban adolescent to the plains of Kansas or the hills of Missouri.

Many of the Christian colleges with the largest enrollments of African-Americans are located in metropolitan areas that have large percentages of people of color in general and African-Americans in particular.[6] In their 2004 study of black enrollment in evangelical colleges and universities, Cross and Slater list the percentages of black enrollment at all 105 colleges in the Council for Christian Colleges and Universities. Not surprisingly, many of those with the largest percentages are located in large metropolitan areas with significant black populations. For example, of the twenty-five schools with the highest percentage of black enrollment, fourteen are located in or near cities. Crichton College in Memphis tops out at 32.8 percent on a list that includes Jackson's Belhaven College (31.6), Detroit's William Tyndale (28.7), Dallas Baptist University (20.5), and Houston Baptist University (19.6). Schools like Eastern University (Philadelphia region), Geneva College (near Pittsburgh), Nyack College (metropolitan New York), and the more rural Wayland Baptist and Indiana Wesleyan benefit statistically from having urban campuses and/or distance learning in cracking the top twenty-five. Visits to their main campuses would reveal far fewer African-American and Latino students in residential undergraduate programs than their overall percentages would indicate.

This is not meant to disparage intentional efforts on the part of these schools. Rather, we point to the reality of recruitment and retention of students and faculty as a challenge when geography and demographics are considered. Schools wishing to increase black student enrollment and faculty presence might want to look at the efforts of other schools on the list in their ability to overcome geographic challenges.

Economics and Prestige: Personal and Institutional

Economic factors affect both evangelical institutions of higher learning and their candidates for matriculation, especially those from historically underrepresented communities. Christian colleges and universities must compete with more affordable public institutions for students in an era of economic recession. They also compete with schools that have a greater endowment and abilities to offer scholarships to the brightest candidates of any color. Hence, they often lose opportunities to bring students into their programs because of financial challenges on both sides.

For the schools with the strongest academic reputations, such as Gordon, Houghton, and Wheaton, this also means competing with the upper echelon of more prestigious (read: better endowed) academic institutions. It is not surprising that the percentage of black students at these three schools would be relatively low on Cross and Slater's list (0.7, 2.0, and 2.7, respectively). Interestingly, Wheaton's enrollment percentage for blacks has been low despite its historic commitment to enrolling black students. Its low percentages of black enrollment may well reflect increased competition for students, as well as economic hardship (as also faced by many historically black colleges and universities, especially the private ones).

When Eastern University began its Templeton Honors College in 1998, Dean Allen Guelzo made a serious effort to recruit African-American students. The Honors College, generously endowed by the Templeton family, sought to provide students attending a Christian college with a challenging academic environment consistent with the best of the Ivies. Indeed, I was Guelzo's first hire as a visiting professor in the program, and he also addressed several groups of black ministers in the Philadelphia area to press the desire for Templeton to have a robust diversity of students in the program. However, the competition for African-American and Latino students came from more prestigious institutions such as Harvard and Yale, and Guelzo was left to lament the slight number of people of color in his school.

Christian colleges and universities seeking to address these financial gaps have their work cut out for them. The identification of targeted funding streams for such development offers promise, but the times are daunting. The same is true for faculty recruitment and retention, as is well documented by Absher.[7] However, her research shows that other factors mitigating against black and Latino faculty appear to be more challenging.

Political History and Race

Significant research confirms what many have known by simple observation: to wit, white evangelicals have been on the "wrong" side of the race issues since the formative years of their schools. While Donald Dayton led the movement to demonstrate nineteenth-century evangelical commitment to racial equality, he also showed how the twentieth century saw that same movement crystallize around the American consensus of racist conventions.[8]

Scores of African-Americans who attended Christian colleges, universities, and seminaries in the 1960s, for example, bemoan the racial insensitivity and prejudice they endured. Psychologist Nicholas Cooper-Lewter details the angst he experienced as an undergraduate at one Christian college.[9] Another pastor told me how he cried in his room on April 4, 1968, while fellow seminarians cheered the assassination of Martin Luther King Jr. These stories accumulate over time to solidify a bias against recruitment efforts, especially by alumni of these institutions. One pastor told me, "I went to a conservative seminary and learned good theology while being treated like a dog. Then I attended a liberal graduate program in religion where I was taught bad theology, but I was treated like a man."

These seminaries' historic failure to attract people of color has been mitigated in recent years by the inability of mainline seminaries to keep their doors open. While some see this as vindication for orthodox theological training, one must wonder whether the black and Latino numbers in evangelical seminaries would have grown in the past thirty years without the closure or relocation of some schools (Philadelphia lost Conwell and Crozer in a period of just a few years, coinciding with growth at Eastern Baptist—now Palmer—Theological Seminary) or the shift in demographics making local seminaries more attractive. A systematic investigation of the growth in numbers seems merited.

The evangelical struggle with race does not always reflect overt racism. Often the culprit is a form of benign neglect—an inability to see the particularity of white evangelical culture and its captivity to middle-class American norms. Calling it "institutional racism" in the 1970s, social scientists have developed a more sophisticated analysis that notes the captivity of most, if not all, forms of white Christianity to the American cultural consensus. White Christianity has also failed to see the diversity of the nation within which American evangelicalism has grown. A cultural hegemony blinds white evangelicals to developing theological norms that include racial reconciliation as a coming together of equals, rather than the adoption of blacks who fit the consensus profile, differing only in color (and gospel music). For example, Shirley Roels notes how evangelical business leaders, overwhelmingly white and male, build their business models, as well as relationships, as though business development is the province of white males with "traditional family structures behind them." Special efforts must be made to see how businesses develop under black leadership in black communities.[10] The same should be true in higher education.

While serving as dean at New York Theological Seminary in the 1990s, I attended a meeting of seminary presidents and deans. One prominent evangelical seminary leader suggested to me that the problem in attracting African-American candidates lay mainly in the weak academic education many of them had received in inner-city public schools. His seminary was developing tutoring programs for inner-city middle school children to address the need for a "stronger pool of academically talented potential seminarians." But this ignores the fact that there are qualities required for seminary education that do not fit the simple academic requirements that evangelical (read: rational orthodox) theological schools desire. If theological education requires spiritual formation and contextual knowledge as well as theological knowledge (as proffered by their accrediting agency, the Association of Theological Schools of the United States and Canada), then some measure for how these factor into admissions ought to broaden the pool in many cases. Nonsectarian colleges and universities, in cases where affirmative-action programs have been phased out, have implemented similar measures to keep a diverse student body a priority.

The Role of Doctrine and Orthodoxy

As referenced earlier in my personal reflections, evangelical commitment to doctrinal fidelity simply does not jell with historic African-American Christian sensibilities. One line from a Negro spiritual says, "You've got to love everybody if you want to see Jesus," pressing the claim that the test of Christian fidelity is action, not doctrine. This is not to say that African-Americans have no commitment to doctrine, but rather that it plays a different role in black churches. Latino congregations similarly invest heavily in an assessment of right behavior in determining what I have called "the badge of fidelity" in Christianity.[11] An African-American congregation may share the orthodox theological commitments of a white evangelical counterpart, but without the central emphasis (read: signed doctrinal statement) that evangelical institutions require.

Hence, colleges, universities, and seminaries that bill themselves as Christian because of their orthodox theology may not come across as Christian to African-Americans and Latinos because of their behavior. Racism and prejudice, insensitivity to cultural context, and ignorance of the experiences of blacks (African-Americans and otherwise) and Latinos often override doctrinal concerns—as was the case for the student quoted above concerning his experience in liberal and conservative schools. It is as if evangelical schools believe that African-Americans and Latinos can "see that they are Christian" based on their doctrinal statements, when both populations are looking for something else. Absher's observations about the comfort level of black and Latino faculty in these institutions are credible.[12]

Absher's research shows that comfort comes in recognizing the need for collegiality amongst black and Latino faculty, as well as recognition of, and credit for, the increased workload of being "community leaders" for the blacks and Latinos on campus. The black/Latino faculty office is a safe place for those students on many campuses, but promotion and tenure seldom recognize this critical contribution. This is a place where the love ethic reflects the badge of fidelity in these traditions. But as long as the rational, reactionary concerns of doctrinal fidelity receive higher billing, black and Latino faculty receive little institutional affirmation or incentive to create this type of supportive space.

Interestingly, many evangelical institutions of higher education have community service requirements for graduation. Such activities—whether deemed curricular or cocurricular—place an emphasis on relationship building and personal formation around the delivery of services and advocacy. If a school requires these for graduation, should it not value the ability to perform in such a context as desirous in candidates for admission? Should not the service dimension of the school's offering have a greater place in the public face of the institution? Are these not recruitment opportunities (even at the middle school level) for these institutions as they wrestle with "true Christianity"? Or are they add-ons to the "real meat" of the school, namely, rational theological principle, whether as the center for theological vocational preparation (seminary) or the context for participation in the marketplace (undergraduate education)?

Historic and Contemporary Mission

All institutions of higher education struggle with the concept of mission. One must consider, first, the institution's historic mission, specifically the reasons for its establishment; second, the influence of culture on mission development—especially the growth of the preprofessional ethos of undergraduate education; and, third, current efforts by administration and faculty to define mission in light of current challenges, including the economics and demographics referenced above. Ethnic diversity struggles to compete with these more "important" mission values, which not only reflect the school's DNA, but also drive its fund-raising efforts. The historic mission of some schools reflects denominational needs, and if the denomination has not made ethnic diversity a priority, the denominational school will have a difficult time making it a priority. When serving as a consultant to one evangelical seminary on the East Coast, I was part of a team (on which were also the school's president and dean) to recommend that the school invest heavily in developing night and weekend programs for second-career graduates coming out of a local evening baccalaureate program operated by an evangelical college. Virtually all the graduates of the undergraduate program were African-American. Our recommendation was greeted by an Episcopal voice declaring that "our mission is to train men for ministry in the [denomination deleted] church, not black Baptists."

The preprofessional ethos actually helps evangelical colleges and universities that invest in adult second-career education, as can be seen in the large numbers of people of color in satellite programs of colleges like Geneva and LeTourneau. African-American and Latino candidates for these degrees can take advantage of programs that integrate Christian formation and market vocation. If the school takes its community service component seriously as a key part of undergraduate education, then an ethos has developed at the institution that enables even second-career evening students to raise questions concerning how their preparation for market vocation relates to prophetic vision, advocacy, and social change. Eastern University's graduate programs in the Campolo Graduate School of Social Change represent a noble attempt to institutionalize and regularize a service and advocacy core for this population and others. Alas, such a move has been risky business for Eastern, as many traditional funding streams are encouraged to invest in more "orthodox" versions of graduate and undergraduate education.

Another dimension of mission has to do with how these schools educate white students. The presence or absence of black and Latino students, staff, and faculty should not be a prerequisite for evangelical institutions of higher learning to "get it right." If the love ethic, ethnic diversity, community service, and so on reflect a true dimension of Christian faith, then an institution's white alumni should be examples of Christian higher education reflecting these virtues. One has only to look at Messiah College and its production of alumnae such as Amy Sherman, whose research on faith and poverty has stood at the forefront of the contemporary development of government partnerships with faith-based institutions in addressing poverty, and Kim Lawton, whose reporting for PBS engages issues that affect the least of these, as an example of how evangelical colleges can glory in the graduation of white students who reflect the institution's holistic mission.

Yes, faculty, staff, and administration take risks when they attempt to place such emphases at the center. Money goes elsewhere, traditional constituencies long nostalgically for "the good old days," and some personnel find themselves ostracized by traditionalist pushbacks. (The seminary president and dean cited previously—both white—resigned and now flourish in institutions that appreciate their sense of vision: one holds a prestigious chair, while sharing a national scholar's prize with an African-American historian, while the other has led a dramatic incursion into an East Coast city, dramatically increasing enrollment among blacks and Latinos.)

In the end, I do not expect the institutions of higher education in the American evangelical tradition to move together into a justice-sensitive kingdom ethics, where diversity is a core value of their mission. But some do make the effort. When caring for the demographic, financial, and missional challenges, some are better equipped to serve this present age.

7

BLACKS AND LATINOS IN THEOLOGICAL EDUCATION AS STUDENTS

Orlando Rivera

Background

I grew up in three cultures. Inside my home, I was Puerto Rican. My parents were born and raised in Puerto Rico. I am the fifth of six children; the first three were born in Puerto Rico, and the younger three were born in New York City, which makes me a Nuyorican—an ethnic Puerto Rican born in New York. Inside my home, the predominate language, food, and culture were Spanish. I grew up eating *arroz* (rice) *y habichuelas* (beans—*friljoes* if I were Mexican) *con carne* (meat) at almost every meal. Our music was salsa, and our holidays had Spanish meaning (like Three Kings' Day). When I left my home, I was black, because of my dark skin color. Because I was born and raised in New York, my mannerisms were more American than Puerto Rican, so much so that most Hispanics did not realize that I was Puerto Rican until I spoke in Spanish. One thing that perplexed me was my parents' prejudice against black people. I would tell my mother to look at my skin, but that did not matter because we were Puerto Rican and therefore better than just plain black people. At school, I lived in an Anglo world. The richness of my culture and experience was not called upon in the classroom. Success at school was judged by meeting the standards, Anglo standards, of intelligence. I was given the distinct impression that being Puerto Rican or black would not help me in becoming an educated person, but would hurt. So in order to make it, I lived in three worlds—Puerto Rican at home, black in the streets, and Anglo for school purposes. When I look at it now, I slid into each persona without much thought—it was my normal.

Education was important to my parents. My father never made it out of elementary school, and my mother had to drop out of high school to raise her family (Mami did go back to complete her GED in her sixties, though). I went to public school after a brief stint in Catholic school—kindergarten to second grade. I went to PS 72 (elementary school), JHS 101 (middle school), and Herbert H. Lehman High School. My mother was very involved in my education and attended every parent-teacher meeting. My teachers knew that if they had any trouble with me, my parents would be there to get me back in line. My saving grace was that I did well in school early on and was in gifted classes. While my friends were warehoused in large classrooms, I was fortunate to have committed teachers and motivated classmates. I graduated with honors and made my way to the state university system. I was considered an exception to the rule, not the norm in my neighborhood. Most of my peers who were not in gifted classes never made it to college.

I thought I was prepared for college, but in my first general education classes it was quickly brought to my attention that

I needed help with my writing. I thought I wrote well—I even won a writing contest on why eighteen-year-olds should vote in high school. I did get help with writing, but decided to major in economics in order to avoid having to write too many papers. I knew I belonged in college, but it did not seem that others saw it that way.

I can remember it as if it were yesterday. I went to the registrar's office to inquire about my schedule and was told that there was no record of me at the college. I protested, "I have an ID with my picture, name, and ID number." The student called a supervisor, who was equally stumped. After twenty minutes, the supervisor said, "Let's try something else." She went back to another filing cabinet and found my record. Her explanation was that my records were not in the Higher Education Opportunity Program files, but under regular admissions. That's French for saying, "You, as a black Puerto Rican, could not possibly have gotten into this college by meeting the admission standards without all the programs we have in place for minorities who cannot get into our college on their own merit!"

Thus began my journey in higher education as a minority student. According to a 2007 report in the *Journal of Blacks in Higher Education*, black college students have only a 43 percent college graduation rate.[1] Perhaps my experience at the registrar's office communicated more than just a simple filing error—maybe it was an indication that higher education was not as used to minorities as all the recruitment literature suggested. Well, not only did I belong, but I finished my studies in four years. (All of us children have graduated from college, three of us have master's degrees, and I should complete my doctorate shortly.)

In seminary, I experienced much the same thing as in college, just at a higher level. My professors appreciated my thoughts, but were not impressed by my grasp of grammar. I had to rewrite many papers, and received several letter-grade deductions on papers until I got married. My wife happens to have a masterful command of the English language. Because of her editing prowess, my grades improved, and I grew as a writer. She was my writing center. I did not sense that I was overlooked, but I definitely felt different.

Given the historical graduation rates of blacks and Hispanics, it should not be a surprise that I was one of only a handful of such minority students in the seminary I attended and one of only two who graduated with my class. It was not a hostile environment, but I had to adjust to the environment on my own. I can remember a preaching assignment that I received from the seminary to speak at a church in northern Florida. I accepted the assignment, but was a bit hesitant because this part of Florida was not known for its diversity, and I happen to be interracially married. I decided to call the church to tell them about my "situation." The church secretary greeted me and said how excited she was that I was coming. When I told her about my marital status, she was quiet. I asked, "Is there a problem? Should I still come?" Without consulting anyone, she politely told me that it would not be a good idea to speak at the church.

The seminary and the denomination it represented were not at fault, but I think they should have vetted the situation more carefully. Though I did not hold a grudge against the school or the denomination, I had a distinct feeling that I was not at home. When I looked further into the denominational school, there were primarily white, non-Hispanic males in leadership. They also had several ministry opportunities available for Anglos and very few for minorities. In reality, they did not know how to place minorities in the predominantly Anglo institution that they represented. Upon graduation, I found a ministry assignment in a nondenominational church, but could have easily stayed with that denomination if there had been a place for me.

Currently I serve in a wonderfully diverse Christian institution that serves 3,369 undergraduate and graduate students. By gender, we are 59 percent female and 41 percent male. Our racial/ ethnic makeup is 10.9 percent Asian, 35.9 percent black, 22.8 percent Hispanic, 24 percent white, and 6.4 percent other.[2] As wonderful as that is, we have only a 44 percent graduation rate. Our graduation rate is below that of the Council of Christian Colleges & Universities, which stands at 55 percent. Although we do an excellent job of recruiting minority students, we must find a way forward to help more of our students graduate. The balance of this chapter will give an overview of how we arrived where we are, indicate the reasons for our dilemma, and propose recommendations for the way forward.

Design Flaw

It can be argued that higher education was not designed for women and minorities. Franklyn Jenifer asserts that when the nation was founded, colleges were developed to provide talented, capable leadership that would steer the American colonies to prosperity:

> By the early nineteenth century, there existed a small group of colleges whose students consisted mostly of the sons of the wealthiest and most elite families in the colonies, as well as a few young male students of high promise from middle and lower income families. Most of the latter received scholarships, which they combined with work to pay for their tuition. All of these students were being educated to assume a leadership role in society, and were expected to be gentlemen who were religious, articulate, and analytical (Thelin 23–24; Lucus 108). The new nation now had a new system of higher education that was exclusively for the benefit of white males. No blacks or women needed to apply because none would be admitted.[3]

When looking at the founding of colleges in the United States, it is apparent that blacks and women were not included. In order to remedy this situation, black colleges and women's colleges sprang up, but they were of an inferior quality. Jenifer posits, "These early women's colleges (and colleges for blacks) offered no collegiate-level education, and were essentially finishing schools that offered some high school education."[4]

In February 2010, a *Newsweek* article reported that American universities are accepting more minorities than ever, but that graduating them is a whole different story.[5] Some of the reasons mentioned were that many minority students who were admitted to college through affirmative action and educational opportunity programs were not prepared for the rigors of academic life in college. Rising college costs have also dissuaded minorities from applying to elite colleges, so that they enroll in colleges that are ill equipped to help them make up their educational deficiencies. The lack of money and resources committed to making up for prior educational deficiencies fuels growing disparity in graduation rates. This leads to a situation that closely resembles the state of our colleges at the founding of the nation:

> "If you look at who enters college, it now looks like America," says Hilary Pennington, director of postsecondary programs for the Bill & Melinda Gates Foundation, which has closely studied enrollment patterns in higher education. "But if you look at who walks across the stage for a diploma, it's still largely the white, upper-income population."[6]

When considering a way forward, theological educators must be aware of the historical models that have given us the current educational situation. As we now look to make recommendations to strengthen the recruitment, retention, and graduation of ministerial students, it is important that we do not forget that the issues facing minorities in Christian liberal arts colleges and those pursing theological educational mirror the issues facing minorities in higher education in general. The following are suggestions to help close the gap for those of us in Christian higher education. The first two deal with recruitment; the last four address retention.

Moving Forward

Accessibility

Many minority students work their way through college and are not able to attend traditional daytime classes. Evening classes and online courses will need to be the norm if we are to meet the needs of our nontraditional students. This may include extra assistance for underserved communities, which often face a technology gap. Use of technology has been linked to improved academic performance. A paper published in 1992 by the Brookings Institution stated, "Even after accounting for family incomes and other factors, black students are much less likely to use computers in school than are white students. . . . If computers facilitate learning; our findings suggest that minority students are disadvantaged by their lower use of computers."[7] We may need to add instructional technology as one of our core courses for all students, but particularly minority students.

Flexible Financial Aid

Our colleges need to consider how we offer financial aid. Some students from disadvantaged backgrounds are not ready to take on a full-time load, but do so in order to receive the maximum financial aid. We should consider offering institutional grants to students who need a reduced course load as they develop the habits necessary to succeed academically in college. We must also help minority students understand the implications of funding their education. When I entered college, my parents did not know how to advise me financially. I was fortunate to attend a state school and had only $5,000 in debt when I graduated. Students need to be aware of the difference between a Pell Grant and a Stafford Loan when they enroll in college. Some families in their excitement to have their first family member enroll in college may unwittingly sign up for loans that are too burdensome to repay.

Diversity in Staffing

One of our core values at Nyack College is to be "intentionally diverse." Key to this value statement is our commitment to provide educational access to motivated students from diverse socioeconomic backgrounds. In order to achieve diversity in recruitment, we aggressively pursue minority faculty, so as to have our faculty reflect the face of our student body. The president of the Rochester Institute of Technology, William Destler, has stressed that diversity is vital to its future as an institution: "RIT is committed to diversity and has been working to drastically increase minority hires and student enrollment because we understand that demographics are shifting rapidly and that diversity is one of the essential elements of excellence and an absolute necessity for the future."[8]

Currently at Nyack College, we are making good progress in this area.

	Student	Faculty
Asian	11%	13%
Black	36%	20%
Hispanic	24%	12%
White	20%	54%
Women	59%	46%
Men	41%	54%

This is important because minority students often look for students and faculty from their background in order to feel comfortable. During a recent visit to a Christian college, one of my daughters said, "I cannot go here; it is too white." We must emphasize minority faculty recruitment in order to make the learning environment appealing to minority students attending our institutions.

Recruitment in Minority Communities

Nyack College was founded by A. B. Simpson in 1882 to train and equip "irregulars" to do the work of ministry. By "irregulars" he meant those who had an earnest desire to learn, but did not come from a privileged background. A past president of Nyack College remarked that elite schools recruit "A" students and pride themselves for graduating "A" students. At Nyack College we are open to those who have a desire to learn. If we admit a "C" student and that student graduates a "B" student who is prepared to enter the work force, we have succeeded in our job as educators. Christian colleges must take the risk of recruiting students who show promise and desire for further education, providing them with support services and preparing them to make solid contributions to society.

Boot Camps

Christian liberal arts colleges and theological institutions should be prepared to provide support and encouragement to minority students who are eager and have rich histories, but are not academically prepared for higher education. While blacks have a 43 percent graduation rate overall, 65 percent of Hispanics and 70 percent of blacks graduated from the State University of New York at Stony Brook.[9] Stony Brook's model consists of three strategic actions:

1. Summer boot camps for incoming students enrolled in the Educational Opportunity Program for students who would not have access to college otherwise. Students spend five weeks in rigorous academic classes. The program has two strict rules: no cell phones and mandatory four-hour study halls daily.

2. Free tutoring is provided to the students, as well as a mandatory six-week-long study skills workshop for those in more serious academic need.

3. Students are required to meet with a counselor four times a semester. According to Dorothy Corbett, "We concentrate on the person, the whole person," and ask students to consider "what is going to make [them] happy and successful as an adult."

Christian liberal arts colleges will need to allocate financial and human resources to meet the needs of minorities who are not matched for college work. As the success at Stony Brook demonstrates, graduation rates across majors are enhanced for minority students who receive assistance to make the transition to college.

Mentors

Christian colleges must enlist graduates and other successful minority businesspeople to mentor minority students. I did not have role models in my field to encourage me along my journey. That is why today I give some of my time to let students know that I made do with God's help and they can too.

Franklyn Jenifer counts as one of his greatest pleasures his ability to mentor several men and women as senior college officers:

During my approximately twenty years as a president and a chancellor in both public and private institutions, I have used a structured mentoring program that has produced several college and university presidents. This program consists of two parts—the Cabinet and one-on-one coaching. I am confident that these leaders and the others produced under similar systems will provide the diversity of leaders that the nation's colleges and universities need. I, also, hope that more senior administrators will take on the responsibility and joy of training the next generation of university and college leaders.[10]

As educators in Christian colleges, we too must develop structured plans to develop future leaders, many of whom have not had models of what a successful, meaningful life looks like. We must be willing to make the commitment to invest in future generations who have the potential to contribute to society, but may not be able to do so without our help.

Conclusion: the Christian College as Redeemer of American Education

American higher education began as an enclave to prepare affluent white males to take leadership in society. The Christian college today must prophetically challenge our educational legacy and make room for the educationally underserved in our society. We must evaluate our attempts to make our colleges rank among the best colleges in America if that means only admitting students who have the highest GPA and SAT scores to preserve our ranking. Jesus did not come only to the well, but to those in need of help. I am not speaking of lowering our standards. I am speaking of making room to develop people who may not have had the advantage of a solid education, but are bright and eager to learn. Our minority students are an untapped resource that merits our attention. We have an opportunity to redeem an educational system that was for the few and make quality education available to the many.

8

A BLACK CHURCH PERSPECTIVE ON MINORITIES IN EVANGELICALISM

Ralph C. Watkins

Introduction: The Root of the Struggle and the Beginning of My Journey

The Lutheran Church—Missouri Synod put out a report in 1994 entitled "Racism and the Church," and in this report it raised the question, "Can the church be an effective witness if it doesn't deal effectively with racism?"[1] The report suggested that

> if the church is to proclaim the Gospel of Jesus Christ effectively to a world that is becoming smaller and smaller and at the same time being violently torn apart by racial and ethnic differences, the church itself will do well to pay heed to the counsel of St. James, who said, "But be doers of the word, and not just hearers only, deceiving yourselves," and "show me your

faith apart from your works, and I by my works will show you
my faith." (James 1:22, 2:18)[2]

The implications here are obvious, in a world that suffers from the
legacy and persistence of racism. The church, being an integral
part of that world, has to step up and do something. It isn't enough
to talk about racism, or have litanies and worship services where
we confess that we have been racist and have benefited from
racism, while continuing to allow racism to persist. The above
quote from the report suggests that we are deceiving ourselves
if we don't work at eradicating racism. As a socio-theologian,
indigenous scholar, preacher, and professor at an evangelical
seminary, I want to suggest that we have to attack the core of
the problem. The core of the problem is a Western-based curriculum that is racist and supportive of a racist world order that
privileges the story of the West over the stories of the rest of the
world. My findings are a result of spending my entire adult life
as either a student, an administrator, or a faculty member at
traditionally white institutions of higher education.

I started my journey in higher education as a student at
American River Junior College in Sacramento, California. I
enlisted in the United States Air Force to pay my way through
college. An enlistment that began in 1982 was completed in 1988
with a degree with honors from California State University at
Sacramento. I then went directly to the University of Dubuque
Theological Seminary (UDTS) in Dubuque, Iowa. I worked my
way through UDTS as a hall director and director of minority
student affairs for the University of Dubuque. It was here that
I got my first taste of what life in the white world of academia
was like for a professional. I had been active in the Black Student
Union and Pan-African Student Union in college and always
focused my studies on Africa and the African-American experience, but as a student I didn't realize how peripheral our story

and experience were to the academy. Being close to black studies as a student is quite different from being tolerated by your peers as an administrator and faculty member. When I started my career in academia, the buzzwords were *tolerance, diversity,* and *multiculturalism.* Little did I know that these words signaled the foundation of my long-term relationship with academia as "an outsider within." By "outsider within," I'm referring to a construct defined by Patricia Hill Collins, who asserts that minorities in the academy are never truly on the inside.[3] They are always the "outsiders" within the walls of the academy, as they are not at the center of institutional life.

Black studies, as it was called back in the late 1960s and early 1970s, was my home. Black studies came out of the movement of cultural awareness in the 1960s led by students who realized that their story wasn't being told in classrooms. The first black studies initiative was in 1966 at San Francisco State College (now known as San Francisco State University) under the auspices of Nathan Hare. African-Americans came out of the Civil Rights Movement and began to say it loudly: "I am black and I am proud," and "Black is beautiful." These affirming phrases, when read today, seem trite or clichéd, but at that time they were phrases that needed to be said by African-Americans to themselves. African-Americans had been subjected to a long history in America and throughout the African diaspora that contradicted these affirmations. These words were liberating, and they served as a rite of exorcism. Black wasn't seen as beautiful by the larger culture; while we don't have room here to deal with race, ethnicity, and the aesthetics of beauty, suffice it to say that white was the definition of beauty. To say "Black is beautiful" and to be proud of being black was liberating and revolutionary.

The Black Studies Movement was a call from students, intellectuals, and activists, saying to the academy and the community, "We have a story that hasn't been told, and this story needs to be shared for our benefit and the benefit of others who haven't heard our story of strength and survival." The leaders of this movement knew they had to challenge a curriculum that told only the story of the West. This institutionalized curriculum was founded on the myth of Western Civilization and the "Enlightenment," which implied that prior to the West there had been no "civilization." A European-based curriculum was and is the major tool in the toolbox of oppression. The story of continental Africans and the African diaspora were conspicuously absent from the curriculum of American schools from kindergarten through college. The stories of ancient Egypt, Nubia, Ethiopia, Carthage, Songhay, Mali, and Ghana weren't central to the story of civilization as framed by the designers of a Western-based curriculum. The West was the place of great civilizations, starting with Greece and Rome. There wasn't a word about the source of these late civilizations that came millennia after the ancient and great civilizations of black Africa, including Egypt (Kemet). The void in curriculum forced students to cry out for their story to be told.

As an academic discipline, Africana studies is committed to telling the story of the continent of Africa, black Africans, and Africans in the diaspora from the perspective of Africans. The discipline starts the conversation with Africa, the place where the oldest human remains have been found, and moves the conversation forward from there. In essence, Africana studies is a historically rooted discipline that doesn't believe in starting the story of humanity and civilization in the middle of the story, in Europe thousands of years after the birth of civilization, which is firmly rooted in the history of black Africa. The sad reality, however, is that some forty years later, while classes have emerged, and majors and departments have surfaced, the story of Africa and the African diaspora is still not at the center of institutional life. Most core curricula in seminaries and universities have no requirement for students to learn about the rich history of

Africa, prior to colonization, or the rich African diaspora. The average curriculum talks about the continent of Africa as if it were a country. If you pulled out a blank map of the continent of Africa and attempted to identify five countries, the average person would struggle. We have no sense of the geography or history of Africa.

Who Am I? A Black Scholar Deeply Rooted in the Black Tradition of Liberation

I am the stereotypical brown-on-brown researcher. I am a child of the Black Power, Civil Rights, Black Theology, and Black Studies Movements. My idols are the who's who of those whom conservatives would call radical scholars. I would call them scholars who dared to tell the truth. My idols were thinkers and leaders like Kwame Ture, Moliefi Asante, Martin L. King Jr. (especially after 1965), Malcolm X, Fannie Lou Hamer, Ella Baker, Huey P. Newton, and Angela Davis. As a socio-theologian, I was a student of W. E. B. DuBois, Marcus Garvey, James Cone, Major Jones, Gayraud Wilmore, and Albert Cleage. I considered myself a black Christian nationalist who was destined to make a difference as an extension of the prophetic tradition of the African-American church. I was concerned about the liberation of African people from the oppressive forces of racism. My journey led me to Fuller Theological Seminary, where I came to head its African-American Church Studies Program in 2005. As we were negotiating my coming to Fuller, a central component of the negotiation centered around whether the position would be tenure-track and at what level in the administration the position sat. The position had historically been part-time, non-tenure-track, at the director level, and had been filled in recent years, with one exception, by a current student. So here I came, calling for the position to be at the dean's level, full-time, and tenure-track. The dean of the School of Theology was fully supportive of the position restructuring and led this process to ensure that the position was repositioned in the life of the school.

The reason it is so important to rehearse the negotiation concerning my position at Fuller is that it sheds light on how racism functions in an evangelical institution, even while the leaders of that institution may not necessarily be racist. When Fuller and other evangelical institutions recruit faculty, the thought of tenure-track or non-tenure-track is rarely, if ever, an issue. It would be rare to post an ad for a Bible, theology, history, or ministry position and have it be non-tenure-track. It would be out of the question for a dean, associate dean, or other upper-level administrator either to come in without tenure or to be non-tenure-track. Why is it only in the case of African-American studies that there must be a conversation and negotiation to decide if the position will be at the dean's level and tenure-track? If the person you are seeking, as posted in your ad, has to have the same credentials as all other faculty, then why the negotiations and questions? What is it in the institutional ethos that favors and privileges the traditional Eurocentric model as normative and rewards those individuals and positions without question, but marginalizes areas that center on the minority story? Why is there a need to have a supporting argument or justification for equal classification?

The good will of the institution is not what I am questioning. The issue I want to shed light on is that, in white evangelicalism, racism operates institutionally, not personally. I prefer to focus on how sinister institutional racism functions on a systematic level. To focus on institutional racism doesn't free individuals from their personal responsibility to fight against racist practices and to be aware of how they benefit from the privileging of whiteness in the institution. This goes especially for white males, who make up the overwhelming majority of the leaders of our institution, many of whom have achieved their positions without having to compete in a national search, which denies minorities the opportunity even to apply for the job. I want to shift the focus because I have not found it very helpful to go around labeling people as racist.

What is helpful and healing is to recognize how the construct of race and the privileging of whiteness operate in the very systems of an institution and produce a bias that rewards whiteness and regards anything that isn't white as *other* and therefore something to be marginalized or tokenized. It is like the classic conversation of "contextualized" theology. Black theology, liberation theology, Latino theology, and feminist theology are considered "contextualized," but Eurocentric theology is not considered contextualized. The theology of the others is not considered worthy of required learning for students in evangelical seminaries. Students are required to take systematic theology, and in these courses they may take note of "minority" theology, but the minority voice is nowhere equal to the dominant Eurocentric voice. The marginalization of voices in text selection, theological discussion, and the very design of the curriculum is a product of institutional racism. Institutional racism consists of all the practices that are embedded in the life of the institution that privilege whiteness. It results in racist acts that use power to act out their bias as they reward one race at the expense of others—and minorities experience a collective discrimination as the institution goes about its daily work.

Life at Fuller: Fully Evangelical and Racist at the Core?

The core of an academic institution is its curriculum. It isn't the faculty, but rather what the faculty teach. A place like Fuller, an institution that I love, celebrates its racial and ethnic diversity. But do we have curricular diversity?

On one occasion, I was sitting with one of my students, and, as I always do, I asked him what classes he was taking, who his professors were, how he was being shaped by his classes, and, finally, what he was reading. This particular student was enjoying his church history class. I asked him what he was reading, and he shared the author's name and book title. I replied, "I read that same book when I took church history twenty years ago." The student replied, "Well, I guess church history hasn't changed that much." We then had a spirited conversation about church history, specifically the African roots of church history, about which this bright student knew very little. As the conversation continued, I realized that there are some things about church history that haven't changed in twenty years: what we teach and what we don't teach. As I talked to this student, I shared with him that I had just returned from doing field research in Ethiopia, and I explained how I was floored by what I saw and learned. The rich church history in Ethiopia was ignored when I took church history twenty years ago, and it is ignored today. What counts as church history has not changed, but it needs to change. When the rich history of the African church is ignored, this is a product of institutional, curricular racism.

When I took church history, we used Kenneth Scott LaTourette's two-volume *History of Christianity*. In the first volume, LaTourette moves to the Greco-Roman world in just nineteen pages.[4] Where is Africa? How did LaTourette miss Matthew 2:13–15:

> When they had gone, an angel of the Lord appeared to Joseph in a dream. "Get up," he said, "take the child and his mother and escape to Egypt. Stay there until I tell you, for Herod is going to search for the child to kill him." So he got up, took the child and his mother during the night and left for Egypt, where he stayed until the death of Herod. And so was fulfilled what the Lord had said through the prophet: "Out of Egypt I called my son."

Out of Egypt! Did he say "Out of Egypt," or could we say, "Out of Africa I have called my son"? If God called his son out of Africa, where he had been for his developmental years, we have to start the history of the faith in Africa. Our faith is rooted in Africa. Thomas Oden puts it succinctly when he says, "Early Christianity tells an historical narrative from the very beginning, from Joseph to Moses to the exodus to the flight of the holy family to Egypt to the Ethiopian eunuch. These are African events that define the whole subsequent narrative of salvation history in the Christian view."[5] According to Oden and the Bible, the Christian story is rooted in an African story. Why does LaTourette pay so little attention to this part of the story? Why do we start in the West when the faith was born in Africa? When LaTourette mentions Egypt, he seems to argue that it was through the Greek-speaking elements of Alexandria that the faith took hold in Egypt, but he alludes to the fact that prior to the fifth century the faith had taken hold amongst native speakers.[6] But was it that late or that simple, and does Africa owe its salvation to the Greeks? If the faith comes out of Africa (Matt. 2:13–15), the question has to come back to us: "How did the faith develop in Africa from the very beginning?" Jesus, Joseph, and Mary had to have some lasting effect on the Egyptians, and vice versa. Did the church begin to develop in Africa? Oden says, "A century prior to the First Council of Nicea (325), these African churches were firmly established, courageously led, actively growing and vital worshiping communities."[7] If we put Oden in conversation with LaTourette, we have a problem. Oden claims that the church was developed—strong, growing, and vibrant—in Africa prior to the West.[8] If we move from Egypt over to Ethiopia, we have a new set of questions: "The Ethiopian Orthodox church has existed in the heart of Africa even before the church began in many parts of Western Europe."[9] Where is this rich history of the Ethiopian church?

We can't run by the text in Acts and not think about what this meant for a nation. In Acts 8:26–40, there is the Ethiopian eunuch, who was sent by Queen Candace to go and worship in Jerusalem. On his way back to Ethiopia, he was met by Phillip and led to the Lord. There are two things this story sheds light on. The first is the queen's religious heritage and connection with Judaism; she obviously was a Jew or supportive of the faith. Second, the eunuch must have done something with his Christian faith when he returned to the queen. In Ethiopian church history, the story goes that Queen Candace was converted and led her nation to Christ.[10]

This was long before Constantine, yet in LaTourette's book the Ethiopian eunuch and Queen Candace are only a passing reference. This rich African history deserves more than a passing reference in Christian history. This is a central part of our story. Why is the story of Africa as the root of Christianity ignored or marginalized? When we trace the history of the church and dismiss Africa, we miss the birth canal of our faith. Thomas Oden says, "The Christians to the south of the Mediterranean were teaching the Christians to the north. Africans were informing and instructing and educating the very best of Syrian, Cappadocian, and Greco-Roman teachers.[11] The flow of intellectual leadership in time matured into ecumenical consensus on how to interpret sacred Scripture and hence into the core of Christian dogma."[12] If the flow of teaching was from the south to the north, why is it that in our educational institutions, such as evangelical seminaries, this African story isn't amplified? How can LaTourette get to Greece in nineteen pages? It may appear that I am chasing rabbits with this argument, but the rabbit is the point. In the curriculum, this omission says that Africans and people of color aren't important. This type of *ignor-ing-ance* is common in the academy, and it is racist at the core. The example

I share is one of many that I could share. We have to take some questions to the curriculum:

- What is missing?
- What isn't being told?
- What is being overlooked?
- What is the color of the curriculum?
- Why don't we take time to do the research and tell about the African roots of the Christian story?
- Is it an institutionalized, systemic, racist act when scholars use their power to teach a theological and historical worldview from a white, Western, Eurocentric perspective that ignores two-thirds of the world's history? Is this institutional racism at the core? Do you get my point?

Moving Forward: The Change That Must Occur Is at the Core

The distinction between institutional, systemic racism and personal racism is a subtle one, but it has to be made if my story is to be heard and appreciated—and if my white colleagues are to be protected and respected. In many ways, my white brothers and sisters are held hostage to evil they don't even know they need to exorcise. And many of my African and African-American brothers and sisters are held hostage by residual racism when they achieve positions in the academy, but don't fight to reform and restructure an inherently racist institution. In evangelical institutions that are grappling with the work of people like Christopher Jenkins and Soong-Chan Rah, the question is still about how they respond to the challenges their work brings to the table. It was Philip Jenkins who sounded the alarm, when he said, "Over the last century . . . the center of gravity in the Christian world has shifted inexorably southward, to Africa and Latin America. Today the largest Christian communities on the planet are to be found in those regions."[13] Soong-Chan Rah proclaims, "By 2050, African, Asian, and Latin-American Christians will constitute seventy-one percent of the world's Christian population."[14] These numbers do not take into account that a majority of Christians in North America will be nonwhite. Global Christianity is clearly nonwhite. At Fuller, how has this reality changed our curriculum? How does the curriculum shift? Where is the center? How can a school like Fuller not have *required* courses, which are at the core of the institution, in African Theology, Latin American Theology, and Asian Theology? Why is it that we are teaching one-third of the theology and history that students and leaders need in a global world?

This takes me back to my central point: at the core of institutional racism is the curriculum. My experience as a chair of an Africana studies department has been one of dismissal. Not only am I seen to have only "black" knowledge, but that knowledge base isn't even respected as deserving a place at the center of the theological conversation. As Christianity throws off the dominance of white theological colonialism, the curriculum remains the same—but it appears that God is doing his own thing by sponsoring a revolution from the ground up. If evangelical institutions want to get on board with what God is doing, they are going to have to change. Evangelical institutions must become students of the world and not teachers of the world. We must let go of our arrogance and move to a posture of submitting to what God is doing in Africa, Asia, and Latin America. We don't need missionaries to come from Africa to America, but we need white, black, brown, and yellow evangelicals to go to Africa and become students. What white institutions have ignored and considered inferior or even pagan may be the very thing that can save them. The question is, do these institutions want to be saved? If they want to be saved, they must ask the question, What must I do to be saved?

First Steps

The first thing they must do is start the historical project at the beginning of the story. They must ask, "If God was in the beginning, and we know that Africa was the beginning, then how was God acting in Africa?" (cf. John 1:1). Second, they must radically change the core curriculum and reeducate their present core faculty about the history and theology of ancient Africa, the African diaspora, Asia, and Latin America. Those of us teaching in seminaries were all victimized by a Eurocentric, racist curriculum. We need to be thoroughly retrained. This training needs to be in the form of yearlong study initiatives, where faculties are required to read and write from the center of history and theology. The reading and writing initiative must include a complete overhaul of the curriculum—an overhaul that throws off the hegemony of one story by putting it in conversation with the larger, more complete story of two-thirds of the world.

A student who graduates from an evangelical institution who does not have a working knowledge of two-thirds of the world's religious and theological history is a student who is ill-equipped to share the gospel of Jesus Christ effectively in a world that is shrinking. The curricular change should be one where we admit that we all are doing "ethnic" studies. Let's identify those centers as such and have pluralism in the academy that demands that students learn the depth and breadth of the human story across seven continents.

The academy must divest itself of the xenophobic, ethnocentric project that promotes white might and the worship of whiteness. Until we decide to stop participating in idolatry, we will never be all that God intends for us to be. We can educate our students to transform the world, but if we educate them in the way we have always educated them, then there will be no change. Are you willing to be reeducated for the sake of the gospel of Jesus Christ?

9

THEOLOGY AND CULTURAL AWARENESS APPLIED: DISCIPLING URBAN MEN

Carl F. Ellis Jr.

ALTHOUGH DISCIPLING urban men can be a daunting topic with broad ethnic diversity, my focus will be on African-American and Latino men who live in the 'hood. The two ethnic histories are different, but many of the same principles apply to both groups.

Thugs

A disciple is someone in the process of learning to obey all things Christ commands. A convert is someone who has surrendered his or her allegiance to Jesus Christ as Lord. Jesus commands us to make disciples; Jesus himself makes the converts—this is the Great Commission. If we try to reverse these roles, we end up with a great debacle. Perhaps this explains our ineffectiveness in urban ministry for these last few decades.

When does discipleship begin? The conventional answer has been "after conversion." However, discipleship actually begins when we first engage someone. When did discipleship begin for the apostles? Let's look to Scripture for an answer.

When John the Baptist saw Jesus passing by, he said, "Look, the Lamb of God!" (John 1:36), and in that moment the discipleship process began.

> When the two disciples heard him say this, they followed Jesus. Turning around, Jesus saw them following and asked, "What do you want?" They said, "Rabbi" (which means Teacher), "where are you staying?" "Come," he replied, "and you will see." So they went and saw where he was staying, and spent that day with him. It was about the tenth hour. (John 1:37–39)

Thus, the first engagement is often as simple as a conversation.

Discipleship has two forms—pre-conversion and post-conversion. The first form, pre-conversion discipleship, brings a person to faith in three phases: (1) practical application of God's Word, (2) planting nuggets of God's Word in a person's consciousness, and (3) connecting the dots of the previous two phases to bring the person first to a God-consciousness and then to a Jesus-consciousness.

1. Practical application of God's Word. This can be something as simple as giving someone a cup of cold water on a hot day (Matt. 10:42).

2. Planting nuggets of God's Word in a person's consciousness. This is like planting a seed. As I listen to people, I often hear them making moral judgments, and, by God's grace, they eventually say something that is biblically true. At that point, I affirm the statement and point out how the Bible expresses this truth. They might be Muslim. They may think that the Bible is baloney, but they have to accept this truth because they have affirmed it themselves.

Another approach is to listen to their stories and point them to biblical characters with similar stories. I once encountered a young gangbanger in Baltimore who insisted that God did not understand or care about people like him. I challenged him by asking, "What if I were to show you a gangbanger in the Bible? Would you be willing to sit down and study the Bible with me?" Certain that I would come up empty-handed, he agreed.

I opened the Bible to Judges 11:1–40, the account of Jephthah. His father was Gilead, and he lived in the land of Gilead. If the place where you live is named after you or your family, it's a sure bet that your family is prominent. We know from Scripture that Gilead was married with several sons, but would occasionally "step out on his wife." His dalliance with a "ho" resulted in the birth of Jephthah. Jephthah's half brothers hated him and banished him from his home. Soon he was joined by "a group of adventurers" (v. 3, according to the NIV). I knew from my knowledge of Hebrew that the word translated "adventurers" was *rêkîm*, meaning "empty, unprincipled, or reckless ones." I explained that Jephthah was joined by a bunch of unprincipled, reckless guys. A good translation of *rêkîm* would be "thugs"—not according to Tupac Shakur's definition,[1] but more in the traditional understanding of the word.

I pointed out to this young man that the thugs in Jephthah's group were skilled at fighting; in other words, they were a gang. I further suggested to this young man that perhaps he was a gangbanger because God had made him a warrior by nature. When I asked if he wanted to be a warrior for God, he got interested, and that was the beginning of his journey in pre-conversion discipleship. After a few weeks of Bible study, he realized that Jesus is Lord and surrendered his life to him. Had I begun by asking if he wanted to be part of the Bride of Christ, he would have recoiled. "Bride of Christ" is a legitimate biblical paradigm, but it was not appropriate in this situation.

3. Connecting the dots of the previous two phases, raising first a God-consciousness and then a Jesus-consciousness. God gave us the Old Testament (God-consciousness) before giving us the New Testament (Jesus-consciousness). Although the Old Testament alludes to Jesus in numerous instances, he is not fully brought to light until he appears on the scene in the New Testament. Hence, as is often heard in theological circles, the New Testament is in the Old Testament *concealed*, and the Old Testament is in the New Testament *revealed*. As we bring disciples to a God-consciousness, we must likewise embed previews of Jesus.

Every now and then you will encounter someone like the Philippian jailer, who will ask, "What shall I do to be saved?" (Acts 16:30). Of course, you do not have to take him though the phases of pre-conversion discipleship. Just tell him, "Believe in the Lord Jesus Christ to be saved" (Acts 16:31). However, Philippian jailers are few and far between. Most people we encounter today are far away from the knowledge upon which the call to salvation is predicated.

The second form, post-conversion discipleship, begins when disciples answer the call to repentance, faith, and obedience. It continues in bringing them to maturity and in equipping them for ministry.

Crying Themselves to Sleep

Discipleship also involves wisely applying God's words to our life concerns. This is the process the young gangbanger experienced. His life concerns were related to his identity as a warrior, even though he had not yet articulated it. Life concerns consist of values and/or issues; values are ideas we embrace as our guiding principles, while issues are problems resulting from sin that either emerge from within us or are imposed upon us.

Jeremiah was right when he said that sin emerges from the human heart (Jer. 17:9). However, not all the sin in our lives comes from our own hearts. Some sin and its effects are imposed from outside. I call this "alien sin," and the sin from our own heart I call "indigenous sin." In the context of the 'hood, alien sin and its effects are abundant.

Values become issues when we encounter forces that suppress them. If education is a value for me and I am denied access to it, then education becomes an issue. Issues become values when we embrace them as essential to us. If I embrace the issue of non-access to education, then it becomes part of my identity. It shows up as the I'm-too-cool-for-school syndrome. This is a tragedy we often see in the 'hood. Anti-academics is the prevailing influence in too many high schools because the *issue* of noneducation has become a value.

When discipling urban men, it is always best to allow them to reveal their life concerns at their own pace. Generally, they do not share their deeper concerns at first contact. The woman at the well had no intention of revealing to Jesus that she was looking for the Messiah. Instead, she was defensive and accusatory, essentially saying, "Who the heck do you think you are? We're dirt under your feet until you want something to drink from us!" However, as Jesus addressed her issues, she finally came to the point where she revealed her deepest concern—her desire for the Messiah (John 4:1-26).

Urban men usually share more superficial concerns at the early stages of discipleship. They are usually comfortable in revealing their life concerns in the following order: outer concerns (generally related to events around them), inner concerns (directly related to them), primary concerns (life-affecting or life-distracting), and, finally, core concerns (life-controlling and life-defining).

Men are willing to share their deeper concerns as they gain confidence in the relationship. To gain that confidence, it is important to give them respect and not judge them. It is essential that we apply God's Word to the concerns they choose to share. As they see how God addresses the concerns they reveal, they begin to share their deeper concerns. Many tough guys I have encountered admit to crying themselves to sleep, but they will not reveal that sort of depth until the relationship is rock solid. The process should continue until they reveal their core concerns.

There are three types of core concerns: personal (e.g., loneliness, anxiety, and fear), social (e.g., education, health, and family), and cultural (e.g., what is happening among African-Americans or Latino Americans). When urban men reveal their core concerns, they usually prefer to start with their least intimate ones: first cultural, then social, then personal. Women usually reveal their core concerns in the order of social, cultural, and then personal. As they see how God's Word addresses the cultural and social concerns, they begin to reveal their personal concerns. Incidentally, this pre-conversion discipleship process also works in the suburbs, and I have even discipled Muslims with extremely negative views of the Bible using this approach. Their attitude did not diminish the power of God's Word as it addressed their core concerns (Isa. 55:11).

Our focus on making converts has often short-circuited the discipleship process. In such instances, we do not take seriously the concerns that urban men choose to reveal. We jump to personal core concerns too soon. This is often perceived as invasive and inappropriate, and it hardens their resistance to the gospel; the result is an intensification of the great debacle.

Crack

The 'hood today is not what it was fifty years ago. What we see today is the result of a great meltdown into cultural chaos.

Before the meltdown, there were three value systems existing in parallel, one of *achieverism* and two of *non-achieverism* (Table 1). Those living by achiever values tended to be the working and middle classes. The non-achievers fell into two categories, the underclass and the criminals. The underclass lived by subsistence values, and the criminals lived by nihilistic values. (Nihilism is a belief that nothing is of value, that everything is senseless.)

Table 1: Clash of Values Among African-American—a Representative List

Achiever Values of the *Middle and Working Classes*	Subsistence Values of the *Underclass*	Nihilistic Values of the *Criminals*
AMBITION "Hard work yields getting ahead."	RESIGNATION "Hard work *does not* yield getting ahead."	RECKLESSNESS "Getting over by any means."
DELAYED GRATIFICATION "Tomorrow will be better than today."	INSTANT GRATIFICATION "Tomorrow will *not* be better than today."	PREDATORY GRATIFICATION "Tomorrow will never come."
PRESERVATION OF PROPERTY Personal ownership	EXPLOITATION OF PROPERTY No ownership	DESTRUCTION OF PROPERTY Anti–owner's ownership
TIME ORIENTATION Planning	CRISIS ORIENTATION No planning	MOMENT ORIENTATION "If it feels good, do it."
GOAL ORIENTATION Planning	NEED ORIENTATION No planning	WANT ORIENTATION "If it feels good, do it."

Note: R. Lupton, the president of Family Consultation Service in Atlanta, Georgia, is the author of two of these lists of values, "Achiever" and "Subsistence" (he uses the term "Survivor" for the latter). From a lecture, October 27, 1984.

Comments on Table 1:

1. *Delayed gratification—tomorrow will be better than today.* E.g., an achiever would not spend $1,200 on spinners to put on his hoopdie.[2] He would put his $1,200 toward a more reliable car.

2. *Instant gratification—tomorrow will not be better than today.* E.g., when non-achievers received vouchers for $2,000.00 to help them function for two months after Hurricane Katrina, in many cases the money was gone in two days—spent on Gucci bags, parties, and lap dances.

3. *Predatory gratification—tomorrow will never come.* E.g., many urban young men routinely engage in high-risk behavior, knowing that they may not see their twentieth birthdays. Yet this danger does not phase them. Their primary concern is to "go out in style."

4. *Exploitation of property—no ownership.* E.g., the tragic demise of the Robert Taylor Homes in Chicago is a vivid testimony to the effect of the non-achievers' treatment of property. They were nice places to live at first, but eventually they became jungles.

5. *Crisis orientation—no planning.* E.g., with this mentality, one does not think about paying the light bill until the lights are cut off.

6. *Want orientation—if it feels good, do it.* E.g., a thief does not think of himself as someone who steals. When he sees someone with an iPod, he sees it as his. At this point, the only question is, how will he get his iPod?

The urban men we disciple come from all three value systems. However, the greatest challenge is to disciple men away from the self-sabotaging and self-destructive non-achiever value systems. This is much more complex than leading someone to pray "the sinner's prayer." They may make better decisions after being saved, but without being discipled into wisdom, most options presented by non-achieverism will be poor choices. As Paul says, "He who has been stealing must steal no longer, but must work, doing something useful with his own hands, that he may have something to share with those in need" (Eph. 4:28). This is about a shift in value systems—more than just a passport from hell to heaven.

A bad value system does not necessarily mean bad character, yet self-sabotaging values are too often a way of life in the 'hood. Tragically, the government often funds the subsistence value system through toxic public policy and a misguided welfare system. There are cases of people showing their utility cut-off notice to the welfare office, only to be told to return when the lights actually get cut off. Some urban politicians claim to be our friends, but, like a crack dealer, they often implement policies that keep us dependent. Discipling urban men involves weaning them off this public policy "crack."

Hostility

From World War I through the mid sixties, the 'hood was a community of leadership and institutions. Racial segregation facilitated class integration. In those days, Shanaynay, who didn't know her daddy, could easily have been Condoleezza (Condi) Rice's neighbor. The leaders and trendsetters emerged from the ranks of achievers who saw the issues of non-achievers as problems *they* had to solve. Achievers knew that non-achievers would be used as reasons to freeze them out of social and economic advancement. Hence, they had a vested interest in inculcating achiever values into everyone in the community. The message of achieverism was heard consistently throughout the 'hood, from the church to the classroom to the barbershop.

In 1967, black consciousness swept in and a cultural revolution took place. Within a few months, we went from being "Negros" to "Afro-Americans" to "blacks." The old strategy for success in America, namely, assimilation into the dominant culture, was replaced by a new strategy—identification with black culture. However, when the revolution happened, achiever values were still preeminent. All the early ideologues of blackness, from Malcolm X to Stokely Carmichael, defined blackness in achiever terms. To be black was to be excellent, to have integrity, to be economically self-sufficient, to be well read, and so on. During this time, the influence of achievers continued to be the stabilizing force in the 'hood. They were like the magnesium rods in a nuclear reactor: as long as the rods are in place, the reactor is under control. However, if the rods are withdrawn, the reactor melts down—fusing everything in it.

There are five factors that facilitated the meltdown of the 'hood:

1. *The growing hostility between achievers and non-achievers, beginning in 1963.* Unlike achievers, non-achievers saw no benefit from the great gains in civil rights. As the lifestyle gap widened, resentment of non-achievers toward achievers increased. They attributed the advance of achievers to the assimilation strategy. In this way, they tried to discredit achiever values, and suddenly achievers were labeled "oreos." At one time, Shanaynay listened to Condi, but now she wants nothing to do with Condi and rejects her blackness as illegitimate.

2. *The explosion of gang violence in the 'hood, beginning in 1964.* Gang members tended to be non-achievers; among their prime targets were achievers.

3. Achievers stopped trying to instill achiever values in their neighbors, beginning in 1965. Achievers continued to live by their values, but because of the intensified hostility, they kept these values to themselves. As a result, achievers lost their influence and blackness was redefined in non-achiever terms. This not only affected perceptions in the 'hood, but also affected the larger African-American culture.

4. The dismantling of housing discrimination, beginning in 1965. For several reasons, including the effects of the Civil Rights Movement, the North began to go through a general process of desegregation. The Civil Rights Act of 1964 did not address the issue of open housing, so housing discrimination was among the last vestiges of Northern segregation to fall.

5. The exodus of achievers from the 'hood, 1965–1985. If the schools in the ghetto are degenerating into chaos, your kids are being terrorized every day, non-achievers now reject your influence, and you are no longer forced to live in the 'hood by housing discrimination, then moving out of the 'hood becomes the logical choice. Acknowledging this, African-American achievers began to leave. Their exodus began with a trickle in 1965 and grew into a torrent by 1975, as blackness was redefined in non-achiever terms.

Ghetto Nihilism

As achiever influence diminished, the 'hood became unstable. By 1985, the exodus of the successful achievers was complete, and the meltdown of the 'hood into cultural chaos was well under way. The result was *ghetto nihilism*—a fusion of subsistence and nihilistic values. Ghetto nihilism has evolved into today's strong and influential culture of non-achieverism, victimology, dysfunctionality, dependency, helplessness, hopelessness, and death, causing unacceptable casualties among our young men. In 1985, gangsta rap burst onto the music scene, giving a powerful public voice to the culture of ghetto nihilism, thrusting it into general and popular culture.

When blackness first emerged, it not only was empowered by achiever values, but also was an aesthetic concept. Because achievers fell silent, the concept of blackness degenerated and became driven by non-achiever values. In other words, we went from *black aesthetics* ("black is beautiful") to *black victimology* ("black is ghetto"). Thus, when Barack Obama was running for President, several self-appointed African-American gatekeepers complained that he was "not authentically black"—a perception that was not related to his being biracial. As the head of a stable, two-parent family, Obama was seen as *not black* because he was *not ghetto*.

Achievers and non-achievers have radically different outlooks, as shown in Table 2.

Our Latino brothers and sisters are also affected by the urban meltdown. First-generation immigrants are generally achievers who work hard to succeed. However, because both parents often work long hours, many of their children are left to themselves and become susceptible to the culture of non-achieverism.

"Candy Man"

As followers of Christ, we look forward to "the sweet by and by," but we must wisely apply God's Word in *the nasty now and now.* "Do your best to present yourself to God as one approved, a workman who does not need to be ashamed and who correctly handles the word of truth" (2 Tim. 2:15). "Handling the word of truth" presents a picture of dishing out or applying; handling the word correctly and unashamedly is essential if we are going to disciple urban young men.

Table 2: Divergent Outlooks of Achievers and Non-Achievers

How they view:	Achievers	Non-achievers
Social justice	Equal opportunity	Equal results
Barriers to success	Mostly internal	Almost exclusively external
Basis of success	The actions of oneself	The actions of others
Effect of values on the poor	Non-achiever values hinder them.	Achiever values oppress them.
Self-destructive behavior	It is acting irresponsibly.	It is the fault of society.
Effect of civilization	It humanizes.	It dehumanizes.
Relationship to the social situation	One is independent of it.	One is determined by it.
Posture toward society	Contribute to it.	Critique it.
Unacceptable behavior	Criminal behavior is wrong.	"Civilized" behavior is false.
How to gain respect	Earn it.	Demand it.
Responsibility	Personal	Institutional
Motivation	Personal initiative	Institutional compensation
Self-destructive behavior	Simply destructive	Reflection of oppression
Who must change	The individual	The society

Note: From a personal conversation with C. S. Morton, pastor of New City Fellowship in Lancaster, Pennsylvania, on July 1, 2010. This is based on his work with identity and value sets.

Principles

The following are four basic principles that can be used in discipleship relationships.

1. We must know the ultimate author of the Scriptures, the Holy Spirit (2 Peter 1:20–21).

2. The meaning of the Bible is its application to life; apart from that, it does not say anything to us.

3. God not only reveals himself in the words of the Bible, but also gives us revelation in the basic patterns of the biblical life situations. Too much theology today tries to extract principles from the biblical narratives, but virtually ignores the narrative itself. What is beautiful about the Scriptures is that the story itself is also revelation. Years ago, Sammy Davis Jr. popularized a song called "The Candy Man." A few of the lines went:

   > "The candy man makes everything he bakes satisfying and delicious,
   > . . . .
   > *You can even eat the dishes."*[3]

   In this discipleship process, the principles are the candy, and the narratives are the edible dishes.

4. There is no life situation whose basic pattern is not already revealed in the Scriptures. Therefore, every person in the urban context has a potential biblical "paradigm partner" with a similar life experience. If God just wanted to give us the principles, the Bible would be the size of a tract. On the contrary, God imbeds these principles in the stories of messed-up people like you and me, some of whom live in the 'hood.

Steps

Here are four steps to a refreshing application of Scripture.

1. Read the Bible and become thoroughly familiar with the narratives. If someone asks you about Mephibosheth, for example, you should be able to tell his story and context without hesitation.

2. Prayerfully look for the basic patterns in your or your disciple's life situation. This is how I was able to get through to the young gangbanger. My professors at Westminster Theological Seminary never taught me that Jephthah was a gangbanger, but they did give me the tools I needed to discover this.

3. When the biblical situation is similar to yours or your disciple's, prayerfully match them up. This does not mean that the paired stories will end the same way. It does mean that you will gain wisdom from your biblical paradigm partner on how to handle the current situation. For example, I was once embroiled in a Saul-and-David situation (1 Samuel, chapters 18–26). David became my paradigm partner and gave me a much-needed understanding of my predicament. My story was not exactly like David's, but through him I gained wisdom on how to navigate this minefield in a godly way. We must learn to do the same for ourselves and our disciples.

4. Once you have matched up the situations, go to the Scriptures and prayerfully look for how God was (a) in control of the situation then, (b) speaking through the situation then, and (c) present in the situation then. All three of these dimensions will be clear in Scripture, forming a solid framework for understanding how God is (a) in control of the situation *now*, (b) speaking to the situation *now*, and (c) present in the situation *now*.

"You da Man"

The Bible itself uses this basic-pattern approach. Examples of basic patterns include the illustrations of Jesus, the apostles, and the prophets. In Isaiah 5:1-2, for example, God says:

> I will sing for the one I love
>   a song about his vineyard:
> My loved one had a vineyard
>   on a fertile hillside.
> He dug it up and cleared it of stones
>   and planted it with the choicest vines.
> He built a watchtower in it
>   and cut out a winepress as well.
> Then he looked for a crop of good grapes,
>   but it yielded only bad fruit.

You can hear God singing this blues song about his disappointment with Israel. Can you almost hear B. B. King in the background?

A classic example of this basic-pattern approach is seen in 2 Samuel 11-12. King David should have been out fighting with his men, but he decided to stay home and kick back for a while. Bored one night, he ventured onto his back porch and spotted Uriah's voluptuous young wife, Bathsheba. David invited her up to his place for a Bible study, which quickly turned into "physical therapy"—resulting in Bathsheba's pregnancy. David attempted to cover up his sin by having Uriah killed and marrying Bathsheba, but Nathan, the prophet, deftly exposed him. Without revealing the guilty party, he told David a story of injustice in his kingdom with the same basic pattern. When David got angry and wanted to kill the guilty party, Nathan said, "David, you da man." Nathan got the word into David before he realized it, and, as a result, David had no defense.

Sometimes discipleship requires that kind of wisdom in the use of biblical narratives. Other examples of the basic-pattern approach are found in the books of Proverbs and Ecclesiastes.

"U Bab"

Think about the woman at the well. Contrary to popular opinion, she was, I believe, a basic "sister" trying to survive in a hostile context. Her problem was that she had never met a real man before—all she knew were males. Jesus was the first real man she had ever encountered, and she didn't know what to do with him. If this were today, she would be in a cult. What would you do after the pain of five abusive marriages and five messy divorces, and if you needed the covering of a man to function in society? She sought covering while trying to minimize the pain.

The Scripture also tells of Nehemiah, living large far away from his 'hood, namely Jerusalem. His position was like that of chief of staff at the White House. However, his heart was back in the 'hood. Jerusalem had once been a nice neighborhood, but it had gone through a meltdown. When his brother Hanani came for a visit, Nehemiah wanted to know what was happening in Jerusalem. Hanani told him the situation was not good—the walls and gates were "jacked up" and lay in ruin (Neh. 1:3). Nehemiah went back to Jerusalem and empowered his people to get a better life. Sanballat and Tobiah were oppressing the Jerusalemites, and the condition of the walls and the gates was testimony to their oppression. However, the oppression also masked their real problem of internalized oppression. The Jerusalemites' revealed concerns revolved around the poor condition of the walls and gates. Nehemiah wisely took these concerns seriously and acted on them.

Oppression is imposed sin (alien sin). In the process of oppression, the sin of the oppressed (indigenous sin) is driven beneath the surface. When the oppression is lifted, the indigenous sin of the formerly oppressed returns to the surface in all its ugliness. This was the case for the people of Jerusalem in Nehemiah's time. Their real issue turned out to be Jew-on-Jew exploitation. The rich were in cahoots with the governor, who levied heavy taxes on the poor. When the poor could not pay up, they had to sell their cattle, then their land, and finally themselves as slaves to the rich to pay these taxes. The rich who bought these families would sell the young girls to Gentiles as sex slaves. The Jerusalemites had to begin the process of liberation from oppression before they realized the seriousness of their indigenous sin. In this case, liberation was a form of discipleship.

Consider this: Daniel, a minority achiever in a superpower, went to U Bab (the University of Babylon) on scholarship as a token Jew. God used Daniel and his friends as a powerful witness to the world (Dan. 3–4). Babylon was eventually conquered by Persia. Under the Persians, Daniel was appointed prime minister because he was best qualified for the job. Some powerful, prejudiced, petty Persian politicians assumed that Daniel was appointed because of a shortsighted affirmative action program. They tried to oust Daniel by digging up dirt on him. When he came up squeaky clean, they surreptitiously crafted the Cat Food Act and used trickery to get it signed into unchangeable law. This law was designed to force Daniel to violate his oath of office as prime minister or compromise his relationship with God. Of course, Daniel's loyalty to God trumped political correctness. As soon as Daniel acted on his devotion to God, the SWAT team raided his apartment, arrested him, and quickly arranged for his execution by cat. However, God turned the tables on the sponsors of the Cat Food Act, and they became cat food themselves.

These are among the many narratives that directly relate to young urban men. That the Bible purposely leaves out some details from the original narratives allows us to recognize ourselves in them in terms of basic patterns. God himself must have the final say in the way we apply his Word, and in this way Scripture comes alive for those we disciple.

Drive-By

Once we have a framework for understanding how God is in control, speaking and present in our situation, we can begin to fill it in with some details. To do this, we and our disciples must go through what I call the "theological process"—a process based on questions.

Jesus said, "I tell you the truth, anyone who will not receive the kingdom of God like a little child will never enter it" (Mark 10:15). Little children are known for asking questions. The theological process begins, first, by formulating our questions. Second, we should ask God the questions we have formulated. Third, we should go to Scripture for the answers. For example, while I was attending Hampton University, the Black Consciousness cultural revolution broke out. At the time, I believed that only Paul's letters applied to us in the "church age." I soon discovered that Paul did not help me in the new cultural context. In desperation, I started reading the whole Bible from Genesis 1:1 onward. When I got to the Prophets, I was surprised to discover that they addressed the same issues of concern to the black militants, such as justice, oppression, and so on. Soon an angry militant confronted me and said, "I don't want to hear about Jesus until you tell me what he has to do with the black revolution!" I now had my question, and I asked, "Lord, what do you have to do with the black revolution?" Then I went to the Scriptures for the answer. Since "all Scripture is God-breathed" and "useful for teaching" the truth, "rebuking" error, and "correcting" faults (2 Tim. 3:16), God used his word to correct my question from "What does he have to do with the black revolution?" to "What does the black revolution have to do with him?"

The fourth step in the theological process is to meditate on the Word of God day and night until God gives the answer to the corrected question. In my example, God began to answer the corrected question in May 1969, at 3:30 a.m. The burst of clarity was so powerful that it grew into my first book, *Beyond Liberation* (renamed *Free at Last?*), and I am still gaining insight from that initial burst today.

In the fifth step, we come back to the situation and apply the answer God has given. When this is accomplished, we have just done theology. Producing theology results in step six (figure 1).

Theology is something we do, not just something we study. When we apply the God-given answers, new questions emerge and another round of the theological process begins. Each time we go around, we fill in more of the frame's details.

This process will make you a theological pharmacist, with tailor-made prescriptions for you and your disciples. What would you think of a drugstore that dispensed only aspirin for every known malady, from headache to cancer? Unfortunately, this one-size-fits-all approach is characteristic of many of our evangelistic efforts.

Figure 1: The Theological Process

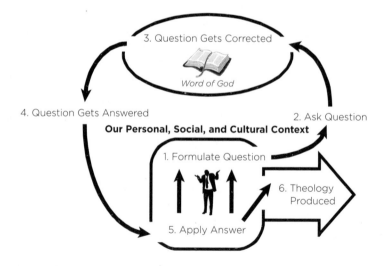

The Bible itself is like powdered milk.[4] It has all the ingredients of whole milk, but it is undrinkable in its present form. You could spoon the powder into your mouth, but that would be problematic. God calls us to make the Bible drinkable by applying the water of our lives to it. If we are going to disciple urban men, we must take the pre-conversion stage seriously. This requires a long-term commitment, not a microwave approach like passing out tracts. That is nothing but drive-by evangelism—not very effective. Urban men do not need another flash in the pan. It might take months before they even take you seriously. They may at times turn away from you in the process, and it may take years before they come to faith. Be patient and prayerful. Remember, it took Jesus three years to bring his disciples to faith.

Finally, to be successful in discipling urban men in the post-conversion stage, you must:

1. Always point them to Jesus as Lord and Savior. They will be tempted to look to you as their savior, and this must be avoided at all cost. It is also good to remember that the discipleship process is often a long and winding road. We must disciple the way Jesus did, leaving room to fail and grace to recover.

2. Remember that you cannot do pre-conversion or post-conversion discipleship in your own strength. The Holy Spirit, through the Word of God, will do the heavy lifting in the life of the disciple; they are both more than adequate for the task.

You may start with many and end with a few. Jesus had five thousand disciples at one time, but 4,988 dropped out because of his hard sayings (John 6:25–70). However, the remaining twelve turned the world upside down, and it will only take a few to turn the 'hood right side up.

AFTERWORD

Anthony B. Bradley

AS I MENTIONED in the introduction, the challenge with this book is to get readers to be willing to listen to someone outside their tribe. We hope that you were able to do that. I've spent nearly twenty years in the theological space of the Reformed tradition. I have also been privileged to have my theological thinking sharpened and challenged by those outside the Reformed tribe. It is our hope that readers will take the stories and hopes of these leaders seriously, especially those who are outside our representative tribes. I am afraid that if we do not, we will not see our blind spots, will repeat the same mistakes, will waste time and resources reinventing the wheel, and will not make much progress. In fact, in the discussions of race, for those of us born after the Civil Rights Movement, the discussion is focused, not so much on reconciling past oppression, pain, tensions, and grievances, as on moving forward—putting on display before a watching world how the gospel creates the platform for racial solidarity (Gal. 3:28).

What is racial solidarity? Two of my heroes who have promoted racial reconciliation after the Civil Rights Movement are J. Deotis Roberts and John M. Perkins.[1] In different ways, these two men both wanted to see the church of Jesus Christ establish a new era of racial unity and peace. While there has been much progress, many of their dreams have yet to come true.

But I am convinced that the church will be able to lead society on race only if it moves beyond reconciliation and pursues racial solidarity, which means embracing our common human dignity (Gen. 1:26–28) as a human family in ways that celebrate and respect differences between ethnic communities for the common good. This goes beyond the failed concept of "color blindness" and recognizes the importance of racial, ethnic, and ideological differences as a catalyst for loving our neighbors well (Matt. 22:36–40; John 17).

I believe that racial reconciliation has largely failed to produce what both Perkins and Roberts have desired for four reasons:

1. Racial reconciliation fails to interrogate white privilege. There is no denying that the dominant cultural group in America is Caucasian. Being a white person in America comes with many unarticulated advantages. In 1988, Peggy McIntosh launched a national discussion by suggesting a framework to engage this discussion—a topic that many evangelicals have yet to explore.[2] White privilege has been defined this way: "A right, advantage, or immunity granted to or enjoyed by white persons beyond the common advantage of all others; an exemption in many particular cases from certain burdens or liabilities."[3] Racial reconciliation does not help whites or minorities explore how the gospel applies to the burdens of being a nonwhite person in evangelicalism. For example, when I joined the Presbyterian Church in America in 1994, I had to wrestle with charges that I had abandoned my race. Many of my white friends had to explain only theological differences to their previous church communities. The fact of white privilege is not the basis of attack, envy, or dissension. On the contrary, the point of discussing white privilege is to help whites see how God can use those advantages and freedom from certain burdens as a platform for blessing those without them. In other words, whites may be missing opportunities to use their privilege redemptively in the broken world.

2. *Racial reconciliation often advances according to the limitations of white social norms.* Because there is little discussion of power in relation to white privilege, minorities are usually put in positions where they have to check their ethnicity at the door in order to engage.

3. *Racial reconciliation does not advance or advocate whites submitting to minorities in authority.* Evangelicalism remains one of the few places in America where racial disparities in organizational structures seem no different from in the era of Mad Men. But much of this is simply a consequence of scarcity. One of the aims of this book is to give ethnic leaders uninhibited freedom to help the church.

4. *Racial reconciliation misunderstands homogeneous ethnic churches as outmoded.* This has much to do with many whites denying that they have cultural norms and failing to recognize that ethnic minorities need cultural centers for survival.

Moving forward, if Christianity is to put the difference the gospel makes in relationships on display in our American churches, colleges, and seminaries, then we need a racial solidarity movement that seeks to do at least the following:

1. *Situate discussions of race within an understanding of white privilege.* It is what it is. Instead of denying it, we need to think

creatively about how it can be used for the advancement of the kingdom of Christ and for the common good.

2. *Advance racial solidarity in ways that do not require minorities to conform to white evangelical cultural norms.* Blacks and Asian-Americans are often charged with being "oreos" or "twinkies" because they are perceived as adopting white cultural norms "on the inside." The discussions need to address the tendency for many whites to perceive progress when minorities are more "like us." The central question here is, what does it mean to have racial solidarity in ways that do not involve minorities leaving their cultural norms behind?

3. *Understand that multiethnicity is not necessarily progress.* Evangelicals seem ignorant of Gordon Allport's 1954 "contact hypothesis" criteria in this regard.[4] As a result, many believe the myth that simply having multiple races share the same physical space changes racial attitudes. Allport's criteria demonstrate that racial attitudes change under certain conditions: when races have equal status, common goals, acquaintance potential, and the support of authorities and customs. These conditions have developed and have been empirically tested over the years, but it is rare to find any evangelicals discussing it. While secularists and mainline Protestants have been discussing this theory as it relates to racial integration, I have not found a single article that involves Allport's insights in a discussion of racial reconciliation in evangelicalism. This is troubling for some. If we are not thinking about the realities of group dynamics, it is uncertain how we are to move from racial reconciliation to racial solidarity.

4. *Develop leaders who are not white males.* Again, this was the main thrust of this book. Lists of Christian conference

speakers are great indicators of whom evangelicals consider as leaders. Great progress in this area has been shown by the Coalition for Christian Outreach Jubilee Conference, while good groups like Together for the Gospel still lag slightly behind in displaying Asian-American, Latino, and black leaders as authorities worth following and those to whom others should submit.

5. Recognize the necessity and importance of homogeneous ethnic churches because of the reality of white dominance in American society. So far, Tim Keller, pastor of Redeemer Presbyterian Church in New York City, is the only evangelical I know of who can accurately explain why ethnically homogenous churches are necessary in America in some cases, especially for immigrants. Because of white hegemony, homogeneous ethnic churches provide a safe haven for minorities in a dominant culture that demands conformity to social customs and norms that are not their own. Also, as Keller highlights in a video interview, ethnic churches serve as helpful cultural centers for survival. For many minorities, homogenous ethnic churches can serve as vital preparation and training for assimilating into an American society dominated by whites. Keller notes that homogenous churches are not needed by whites because they form the dominant culture.

Because some may miss the point, I quote Keller here extensively, as he spoke in an interview:

> I actually do think the African-American Churches have more to lose than we white churches do. Now, if you go in the Redeemer, you're going to find that Redeemer is about 45% Anglo, about 45% Asian, and about 10% black and Hispanic. A lot of the churches . . . in the middle or lower Manhattan that are more Evangelical Orthodox Charismatic will have that same kind of mixtures. There are very few white churches around. I'd

say the ethnic churches—which will be the African-American churches or Latino churches, the Asian churches—it is more difficult for them to become multi-ethnic, because in some ways they're community centers for their people and they could lose some of their power in a sense as representing their people to the broader culture. It could be that in post-Obama, there's big questions about the old models for how you do ethnic empowerment, but that's not something for me to speak to, I don't think. I mean, I actually counsel all churches, I say, "You should be as multi-ethnic or more multi-ethnic than your neighborhood."

So, if you live in a neighborhood that is so many African-Americans, so many black, Latino, so many white, you should try, your church should look like your neighborhood. And if you are, you actually do better than the neighborhood because usually out of the neighborhood those groups of people don't mix all that well. They usually alongside of each other may be friendly, but they don't really work together. So if you could be a church that shows how the groups work together, you get, in a sense, be more multi-ethnic than your neighborhood. But, basically, we say be as multi-ethnic as your geography, so I push that pretty heavily. And so, yeah, I would love to see a multi-ethnic future church, but I realize the ethnic churches have a lot to lose, so I'm careful when I say that. I don't want to make them feel that somehow they're doing wrong to stay more mono-ethnic. I still see a role for that. I don't see much of a role for a purely white church anymore, but I do see a role for the ethnic churches.[5]

Finally, in the coming decades, there will be great opportunities to put the multiethnic implications of the gospel on display (Gal. 3:28) as we seek to love our neighbor in ways that Perkins and Roberts challenged us to do decades ago by using new categories to address an ongoing problem. Richie Session's sermon on the implications of Galatians 2:11–14, preached at Independent Presbyterian Church, serves as a good starting point for moving from racial reconciliation into racial solidarity.[6]

Finally, we hope that this book will encourage larger conversations among evangelicals from many tribes and races (Rev. 7:9), as the gospel unites God's people for his glory and the spreading of the gospel as God redeems his world. There will be so many wonderful opportunities in the future for rising generations to do even greater work for the kingdom in the area of race, and we look forward to seeing what emerges in the coming years.

APPENDIX

RACISM AND THE CHURCH: OVERCOMING THE IDOLATRY

A Report of the Commission on Theology and Church Relations of The Lutheran Church—Missouri Synod

February 1994

PREFACE

In April 1986 the officers and staff of the Commission on Theology and Church Relations, at the request of the President of the Synod, met with a number of African American pastors in the Synod to discuss issues related to black ministry and to share matters of mutual interest. Following this meeting, the Executive Director of the Commission on Black Ministry expressed appreciation for this opportunity to exchange ideas and opinions and, at the same time, forwarded a request from black leaders in the Synod that a document on racism be prepared. The Commission on Theology and Church Relations responded positively to this request and immediately placed this study on its agenda.

Calling on all of its members "To Combat All Racism," the Synod at its 1992 convention in Pittsburgh urged "the rapid completion of the CTCR study" and asked the members of the Synod "to make maximum use of this study upon its completion and to pray the Lord of the church to bless this study and cause it to effect appropriate changes in attitudes and actions."[1] The Commission on Theology and Church Relations joins in the prayer that this document on *Racism and the Church* will be a blessing to the Synod, assisting us all not only in understanding the problem of racism, but also, with God's help, in dealing with it in our own personal and corporate life. For those who wish to explore in more detail what the Scriptures teach regarding racism and its consequences, a Bible study has been included with this report (pp. 45–56).

INTRODUCTION

"That to which your heart clings and entrusts itself," Dr. Martin Luther wrote in the Large Catechism, is "really your God." "If any one boasts," he continued, "of great learning, wisdom, power, prestige, family, and honor, and trusts in them, he also has a god, but not the one, true God."[2] If anyone should claim superiority over others and treat them as inferior because of racial origin or characteristics, we may add, that person, too, has a god, but not the one true God. Racism is at its core idolatry—even though, to be sure, it also violates any number of other specific commandments. Racism grounds the identity and security of human life not in the God who alone is our Creator, Redeemer, and Sanctifier, but in self. It is a sin against the First Commandment because it fails to receive other human beings as gifts from God. It is to this malady of the human heart and life that we address ourselves in this report.

By focusing in this discussion on the sin of racism as a form of idolatry we do not imply, of course, that it merits condemnation harsher than other sins that manifest a refusal to cling to God alone and to no other. All sins ultimately have their origin in the failure to fear, love, and trust in God above all things, and they need to be judged as such. For this reason Luther saw the First Commandment of the Decalogue as "the chief source and fountainhead from which all the others [commandments] proceed."[3]

It is important to recognize that the sin of racism, like all other sins, cannot be overcome by human strength or resolve. Of the commandments Luther said, "they are set on so high a plane that all human ability is far too feeble and weak to keep them."[4] Therefore, only by the power given by Christ, who alone is our Deliverer from sin and whose death earned for us forgiveness for all of our offenses, are we able to combat the sin of racism.

As we begin this study, two additional points need to be made. First, in this report we have made use of the African American experience as the primary paradigm for analyzing and understanding the issue of racism in the church. This is not to suggest or even imply that the racism suffered by any other racial group is any less offensive or burdensome than what African Americans have known. There are important reasons, however, for this focus. While the degree of racism against individual groups in American society has varied historically, African Americans since their arrival on this continent have been among the most frequently targeted objects of racism and have suffered some of the most negative consequences of it. With them the problem has been most widespread. Moreover, they are not only the largest single minority group in American society but also the largest minority within the Lutheran church.[5]

Second, since many of the concepts and terms that characterize the contemporary discussion of racism have been taken from the physical and social sciences, we have found it helpful in part I of this document to make use of the language of these disciplines in describing the nature of the problem we confront when we discuss racism. Our purpose in this section is purely descriptive—to define terms and to review some of the concepts widely used by both proponents and opponents of racism today. We believe that this will enable us to proceed in a more informed way in evaluating the tenets of racist ideology on the basis of the Holy Scriptures, the Word of God. This we do in part II.

With these preliminary considerations in mind, we begin our discussion of racism by analyzing in part I the nature of the problem before us. In this section, which includes also an excursus presenting a historical perspective on the issue of racism in American Lutheranism, we offer a definition of racism, present a rationale for engaging the question at this time, and underline the importance of recognizing that racism is an ideology. In part II we set forth the biblical principles that apply to the theological issues raised by racism, and we do so in terms of the three articles of the Apostles' Creed. Part III provides specific counsel for overcoming the sin of racism in the church.

I. RACISM AND THE NECESSITY OF A CHRISTIAN RESPONSE

A. What is Racism?

The church's response to racism is complicated by the lack of agreement among sociologists and anthropologists regarding certain facets of this issue. In fact, there is less than complete consensus regarding the very definition of the term "racism" itself. Our purpose in this study is not to resolve such differences. Yet, to clarify the nature of the problem before us, we need to present briefly a commonly accepted definition of racism and to examine a number of other concepts related to this issue. Differing understandings of how racism should most precisely be defined should not divert attention away from the main thrust and purpose of this document, namely, to offer a biblically informed Christian response to this problem.[6]

I. Definition of Racism

"Racism" has been defined as "the theory or idea that there is a causal link between inherited physical traits and certain traits of personality, intellect, or culture and, combined with it, the notion that some races are inherently superior to others."[7] According to this definition, racism refers to the belief that organic, genetically transmitted differences (whether real or imagined) between human groups are associated with the presence or absence of certain socially relevant qualities or abilities that are determinative of people's social worth and their value as human beings.[8] Racist ideology also makes judgments about people's worth on the basis of their inclusion in nonbiological and nonracial groupings such as religious sects, nations, linguistic groups, and ethnic or cultural groups.[9]

Because racism assumes, explicitly or implicitly, that one human group is better than another in ways that entail superior social or individual value, it manifests itself in actions that adversely affect the lives of others. This is the case especially when those who are in a position to enforce their prejudices use their influence to harm others regarded as inferior, and even to exploit them.[10] Racist thought seeks to justify self-aggrandizement, cruelty, and paternalism in favor of the "superior" group and to inflict low self-image, subservience, deprivation, loss of equal privilege, and even slavery upon the "inferior" group. To be sure, one does not need power to be a racist nor is racism limited to "a majority group." Nevertheless, the misuse of power has been and remains an integral factor in the apparent intransigent nature of racist ideology.

As we seek to understand the various elements of racist thought and behavior, we also need to consider a number of important terms employed in discussions of this issue. We recognize that in practice, as well as in common parlance, these terms are often not clearly and easily distinguished. However, if we wish to take seriously the nature of the problem before us and to engage in a credible witness to what God's Word says about this matter, we should be familiar with a number of terms and their use in discussing the problem of racism. We call attention to the following.

a. Race. One of the crucial issues in responding to the phenomenon of racism is the use of the term "race" itself. This word generally conveys the idea that the human family is divided into a number of biologically distinct groups. The closeness of common descent and shared physical distinctiveness (such as color of skin, hair type, facial features) define one's "racial" identity.[11]

Most anthropologists today point out, however, that human populations constitute a genetic continuum where "racial" distinctions, due to such factors as migration and intermarriage, are relative, not absolute.[12] In other words, traits attributed to race are present on a "more-or-less basis" (e.g., skin color pigmentation) in distinction from other traits that manifest themselves on an "either-or" basis (e.g., blood type group). Social scientists point out that there is far more trait variation within the human species than is visible to the naked eye. Consequently, the biological meaning of "race" has become so problematic that

> some social scientists argue that *race*, as a biological phenomenon, does not exist. Others take the less extreme position that while different races exist, extensive interbreeding in many societies has produced large numbers of people of mixed ancestry.

The assignment of these people to racial categories depends on social, rather than on biological, criteria. Thus the social consequences of biologically inherited traits is the fundamental issue of the sociological study of race.[13]

The studies of anthropologists and sociologists have helped us to see more clearly the difficulties and ambiguities inherent in the concept of "race." But the problem of racism arises when this term is used to indicate that biologically distinct groups (races) differ not only in their physiology but also are inherently superior or inferior in terms of their intellectual capacity, morality, human potential, and social worth. Because such human traits, according to racist ideologies, are biologically determined, they are passed on from one generation to the next.[14] This is a basic presupposition of racism.

b. Culture. The *American Heritage Dictionary* defines "culture" as "the totality of socially transmitted behavior patterns, arts, beliefs, institutions, and all other products of human work and thought characteristic of a community or population."[15] Culture is the "social heritage" of a community.[16] In the judgment of most contemporary authorities, culture is a more useful and scientifically verifiable way of identifying, explaining, and understanding differences among human beings than is race.

Culture is a unique collection of customs and patterns of behavior. But, as many authorities also point out, culture refers not merely to the external social "artifacts" of a community. It is, so to speak, a blueprint within the mind by which people perceive the world, live within a particular group, and adapt to life on this planet. Culture consists of a group of assumptions about the world and according to which one organizes that world, defines, values, manipulates, and responds to that world. Peoples of different cultures not only "see" and "inhabit" different "worlds," but they also have dissimilar feelings about the same universe in which they live. So important is culture that its loss can even jeopardize a person's very physical survival.[17]

The social and physical sciences teach us that it is erroneous to think that culture is merely an accumulation of quaint, if not esoteric, customs that have an equivalent in every other culture. We raise this point because racist thinking often diminishes or even rejects altogether the role of culture in defining the differences between human groups.

c. *Ethnic Group.* A third term and/or category we need to keep in mind when we evaluate racist thought and behavior is the expression "ethnic group." An ethnic group is generally defined in terms of sharing a common language, a common set of religious beliefs, or some other cultural characteristics—but *without* physical considerations.[18] This term designates a group of people who share a common history based on distinctive features and values that are identified with that group. Sometimes the terms "ethnic group" and "nationality group" are used interchangeably. It may be more precise to use "ethnic group" to refer to a group's culture (behavior), and "nationality group" to point to its national origin.

Historically, some of the people who settled in the United States have developed as ethnic groups in a deliberate effort to preserve the identity and heritage they had in their homeland. In other instances, American society has itself actually created ethnic groups even while advocating a policy of assimilation. Two examples may be given. There is the case of the Japanese Americans who, having arrived voluntarily in the United States of America at the turn of this century, eagerly sought assimilation. But, under pressure from all sides—labor unions, the *San Francisco Chronicle*, the city council, and even the state legislature—they were finally driven out of San Francisco, their port of entry. Mostly shopkeepers in Japan, they were forced to take up truck farming to survive. Ethnic group formation was well under way.[19]

African Americans are another example of American society quite literally creating an ethnic group. They did not come from one nation but from many different societies and cultures. They were also physiologically diverse. Unlike the Japanese, however, they did not migrate voluntarily, but were kidnapped and forcibly transported to this country. Even before they were unloaded from the slave ships, concerted efforts were made to strip them of any knowledge of their history, their culture, and their identity as human beings. Slaveholders deliberately attempted to impose on them a new identity.[20] Emerging from this effort at cultural destruction was the ethnic group currently known as "African Americans." It is important to note that the same forces of ethnic group formation that operate in society may also be present in religious institutions.

What we have said here underlines an important distinction that needs to be made between "racial groups" and "ethnic groups."[21] Groupings of people sometimes identified as "racial groups" may in fact be "ethnic groups." The physiological differences among African Americans, for example, are so numerous that it is impossible for an objective observer to identify them as a unitary biological group. This distinction between racial and ethnic groupings is critically important for those seeking a better understanding of the nature of racism and its ideological roots.

d. Ethnocentrism. The term "ethnocentrism" refers to what may be a positive appreciation of and preference for one's own culture. From birth human beings are generally led to believe that their own cultural ways are the best, if not the only way of going about life. People are not only aware of their native culture, but they are also emotionally attached to it. In fact, it is doubtful if any cultural system could survive without some degree of ethnocentrism.

But ethnocentrism may easily degenerate into that "view of things in which one's own group is the center of everything, and all others are scaled and rated with reference to it."[22] This way of thinking becomes problematic when the standards of one culture become the basis for making selections and determining opportunities for people from a variety of racial, cultural, and ethnic groupings. When institutions sanction and implement these standards, forced assimilation and/or exclusion result.

This leads us to an insight that will be helpful to keep in mind for our later discussions of a Christian response to racism: the principle that every culture must be analyzed and understood in terms of itself, not on the basis of another culture. Anthropologists call this "emic analysis."[23] This principle requires, for example, that to understand the Hispanic family system one would have to examine it from within the context of Hispanic culture, not by comparing it with the family system of white middle-class Americans. Emic analysis is of critical importance for Christians who desire to proclaim the Gospel to groups that differ culturally from their own.

e. Majority/Minority Groups. The expressions "majority/minority groups" do not always necessarily refer to statistical groupings. These terms may also be used to designate social and political dominance and/or the lack of such dominance. They have come to convey the following technical meanings: (1) "patterned dominance" which is neither a random nor an unpredictable relationship; (2) a stratification system with a hierarchy of superiority and inferiority; (3) "categorical status," that is, individuals have an ascribed status regardless of what they do in life (castes); and (4) unequal distribution of power. Thus, when someone is referred to as belonging to either a majority or a minority group, this can also be a way of telling them who they are, where they belong in the social world, and how they are expected to behave.[24]

Not everyone who belongs to a "majority group" based on race, of course, actively participates in the subordination of those belonging to a "minority group," applauds such a practice, or even thinks in terms of racial privilege. But there is a broader sense in which everyone in such groups is involved in the problem of racism. Since all are born into their respective groups (one does not choose to join or have the privilege of resigning), racial privileges and liabilities accrue to each individual regardless of his or her choice.

f. Prejudice.[25] Prejudice is an attitude of deep dislike (that is, an aversive or hostile attitude towards an individual or group) based on faulty and inflexible generalizations. It is an attitude acquired without, or prior to, adequate evidence or experience. Unlike a simple misconception, prejudice actively resists evidence to the contrary.

Prejudice also has an emotional component connected with it. It is characterized by a rigid or inflexible attitude or predisposition to respond in a certain way to its object. When the object of prejudice is a group, the individuals included in it may be viewed as a group only in the mind of the prejudiced person despite the fact that its individual members may have little similarity or interaction with each other. Prejudice entails systematic misjudgment of the facts.

Characteristic of prejudice is the tendency to select certain facts for emphasis, while downplaying others. New experiences are made to fit old categories through selection of only those cues that harmonize with a prejudgment or stereotype.[26] Because of their emotional quality, prejudicial attitudes are generally quite persistent and resistant to change.

Prejudice is learned. It is not usually acquired through direct contact with its object, however, but with prevailing *attitudes* toward it. Thus, a prejudiced person's claim to "know" members of a racial "minority group" may be no more than knowledge of prevailing attitudes toward the individuals included in this grouping.

Even though they are intimately related, racial prejudice and racial discrimination are sharply distinguished by sociologists.[27] While prejudice is a psychological or attitudinal phenomenon, discrimination always refers to behavior (particularly *social* behavior). An individual may be prejudiced without necessarily engaging in discriminatory behavior. By the same token, a person may participate in discriminatory behavior that is not necessarily motivated by personal prejudice. However, discrimination and prejudice very often go hand in hand, since each fosters and reinforces the other. Prejudice gives rise to and helps people rationalize discriminatory behavior, and discriminatory actions often produce and/or reinforce prejudicial attitudes toward the objects of discrimination.

g. Power. Power in and of itself is not evil. Every society and institution by definition distributes power according to certain patterns and norms for the maintenance of order and the common good. However, when power is used—whether by a society, institution, or individual—to enforce prejudice against others, that exercise of power becomes evil. When racism involves the misuse of power, it results in harm to the object of the prejudice.

Power can be exercised in numerous ways. It may manifest itself as coercion (even brute force), authority (the recognized right to give orders and have them obeyed), prestige (symbolic and honorific), or sheer dominance (clearly and largely uncontested superordinate power). The misuse of power by those who practice racism may often be more subtle than it is brazen. Easily recognizable is legally enforced segregation. Less detectable is the unassuming imposition of one's will on others, or the advancement of one's own welfare at the expense of others—something still possible even if individual prejudices or hostile attitudes toward another are to a great extent removed.[28]

2. Racism as an Ideology

Crucial for an understanding of the nature of racism and its pervasiveness in our time is the recognition that racism is a belief system. In the words of Alan Davies, an ideology is "life . . . squeezed into the idea, and made to conform to its dictates."[29] As an ideology or belief system racism seeks to provide a rationale to justify racial divisions, and, as history has shown, may even seek to divide and rule society and the world along racial lines. Racism also has a certain coherence to it. It draws conclusions about the nature, purpose, and/or destiny of the human family that are based on the theory that because of biological, hereditary, or cultural differences, other members of the human family are socially or morally inferior.

As an overt belief system racism is now publicly spurned and commonly declared abhorrent in our society. But racism as an ideological reality is, unfortunately, not dead. Quite the contrary, racism in its varied forms shows up at every level of our life today, and it is precisely because it most often possesses "an incognito character" that it is so ominous.[30] It can, and usually does, manifest itself at the level of the *individual*. An individual may act on the belief that members of a group, as a group, are inferior in human or social value simply because of apparent biological, cultural, ethnic, or national differences.

It is possible also to speak of *institutional* racism with respect to the way institutions operate (through their laws, customs, practices, procedures). Here the focus is on how institutions *function*. The term "institutional racism" is not used to question the intentions or even necessarily the behavior of individuals who manage such institutions. In many instances, these individuals may not even realize that a given institution functions to the disadvantage of a given group of people.

Finally, racism may also manifest itself at the level of *culture*. This is the view that all cultures are inferior to one's own culture, and that those inferior cultures consistently produce inferior results. Viewed from a historical perspective, cultural racism is sometimes referred to as "cultural imperialism" or "cultural colonialism."[31]

Excursus:
A Historical Lutheran Perspective

It is not possible to understand the problem of racism in the church today without also placing the issue into the broad historical context of Lutheranism in America. Therefore, after making a few preliminary observations concerning the rise of racism in modern times, we present a perspective on racism in the history of the Lutheran church in America.

The concept of "race" first appeared in discussions at the end of the 18th century, but racism did not gain wide acceptance as a "scientific" theory of behavior until the 19th century, which has been called the age of racism *par excellence*.[32] By the latter half of that century racism was acknowledged as a fact by the vast majority of western scientists, and it was popularized through the writings of such people as Joseph-Arthur, comte de Gobineau, Houston Stuart Chamberlain, Rudyard Kipling, Alfred Rosenberg, and Adolf Hitler.[33]

As an American phenomenon, historians generally agree, the origins of racial prejudice based on biological considerations were closely tied to the practice of slavery and colonial expansion.[34] Europeans promoted racism on this continent in the form of slavery shortly after embarking on their voyages of discovery. As they saw it, slavery was a matter of economic expediency, if not necessity.[35]

What developed as the "American dilemma," therefore, is by no means a recent invention. The founding fathers of this republic not only condoned slavery, they "institutionalized" it by declaring slaves to be three-fifths of a person for purposes of congressional representation by whites, but nonpersons themselves before the law. Thus, racism as a part of the fabric of American society has a long and tenacious history.

In the history of racism, the church did not play the role of the disinterested party, existing in a social vacuum or morally neutral environs. Nor did the Lutheran church in the United States remain aloof or untainted by the racism that became so much a part of American society. Racism within the Lutheran church was essentially no different from that which existed in the secular society. It was subject to the same forces that manifested themselves historically in this country. We may cite as an example the Lutheran church's attitude toward slavery.

When Lutherans who came to American in the 18th century confronted slavery, they were not of one mind on this issue. Some in the Lutheran church opposed the institution. Among the first to do so were the Swedes. When Gustavus Adolphus proposed establishing a colony in the New World, he took the position that the colony would "gain more by free people with wives and children" than with slaves.[36] Other Lutherans, however, supported slavery and saw no moral inconsistency in their stance. In 1708 a Native American, the first slave on record to seek membership in the Lutheran congregation in New York City, caused a crisis. His Lutheran owner protested his acceptance by the church out of fear that he would lose his property. The crisis was resolved when, at his confirmation, Thom promised to "continue to serve his worldly master and mistress as faithfully and truly as if he were yet in his benighted state."[37]

In 1735, when colonial Lutherans formally took notice of Negro slaves becoming members of the church, the constitution of Wilhelm Berkenmeyer, a Lutheran pastor in the Hudson valley, specified that

> a pastor shall previously ascertain that they [Negro slaves] do not intend to abuse their Christianity, to break the laws of the land, or to dissolve the tie of obedience [slavery]; yea, he must have a positive promise that Christianity will not only be entered upon, but that the same shall be practiced in life.[38]

Berkenmeyer, himself a slave owner, evidently saw no contradiction between the principles of Christian ethics and slavery. When criticized for owning slaves, his defense was that it was nobody else's business inasmuch as he had purchased the slaves with his own money.[39] If the Christian faith has anything whatsoever to say about slavery, as far as Berkenmeyer was concerned, the onus of responsibility is on the slave, with no apparent responsibility on the part of the owner.

At almost the same time that Berkenmeyer's constitution was adopted, the first Lutheran congregation in the South (Hebron Church in Madison County, Virginia) sent a delegation of three to Europe to solicit funds. One of the reasons for requesting funds from European Lutherans, as the Rev. Mr. Stoever put it, was so that

> every effort [could] be made to lead the heathen, who still walk in darkness, to Christ [and that those who receive the pamphlet should] send contributions across the ocean for the quickening of the poor fellow believers and the conversion of the heathen.[40]

The committee came back from Europe with $10,000, but there is little evidence that those Lutherans ever used this money to try to lead "the heathen, who still walk in darkness, to Christ." Part of the money was used to purchase slaves to work the land that supported the pastor. By 1748 the congregation owned nine slaves.[41]

The issue of slavery almost led to the destruction of the Lutheran church in colonial Georgia. The Salzburgers (immigrants from Austria) were adamantly opposed to slavery even before they arrived in Georgia in 1734.[42] Part of the agreement signed by every member of the community bound them to reject slavery. Within three years of their arrival, however, the leader of the Salzburgers, the Rev. Johann Martin Boltzius, knew firsthand that at least one of his members, Mr. Kiefer, was secretly housing slaves on his farm.

By 1750 the issue of slavery forced Boltzius to make a decision: either consent to the introduction of slavery in Georgia or preside over the demise of the Lutheran community.[43] Boltzius (a devout pietist) decided, much against his personal convictions, in favor of slavery.[44] By the early 1770s, however, two slaves were listed as part of the inventory of church property (they were Boltzius' personal servants) and two other Lutheran pastors were among the largest slave owners in the community.[45]

Perhaps the strongest statement in favor of slavery by a Lutheran synod was issued in 1835 by the South Carolina Synod when it said,

> Whereas individuals and Societies of the North, calling themselves abolitionists, under the pretense of ameliorating the conditions of our servants, have created an excitement deeply affecting our interest, and calculated to sever bonds of attachment which exist between master and slave; and whereas this unjustifiable interference with our domestic institution is opposed to the Constitution of our common country, is subversive of our liberties as men and contrary to the precepts of our blessed Savior, who commanded servants to be obedient to their masters, and the example of the holy Apostle Paul, who restored to his lawful owner a runaway slave; therefore:
>
> 1. Resolved, unanimously, that this Synod express their strongest disapprobation of the conduct of Northern Abolitionists—

and that we look upon them as the enemies of our beloved country; whose mistaken zeal is calculated to injure the cause of morals and religion.[46]

This was perhaps one of the strongest pro-slavery statements made by any Lutheran body. It is also important to note that an appeal to the teachings of Jesus and to the example of St. Paul was made to justify that slavery. (Cf. pp. 62–64 in the Bible Study of this document.)

Not all Lutherans were so accepting of slavery. Pastor Henry Melchior Muhlenberg would have no part of it, even though one of his sons was a slaveholder. The Franckean Synod was quite forthright in its opposition to slavery. It refused to have fellowship with anyone engaged in that kind of immorality.[47] This was also the second Lutheran synod to ordain an African American for the office of the holy ministry.[48] The president of Gettysburg Seminary, Dr. Samuel S. Schmucker, required his wife to sell her slaves and turned his home on the seminary campus into one of the stations on the underground railroad.

We get a glimpse of what was probably the most widespread attitude of pre-Civil War Lutherans towards slavery at the third annual convention of the Tennessee Synod in 1822 when, in response to a lay delegate's question as to whether slavery was to be considered an evil,

> the Synod unanimously resolved, that it [slavery] is to be regarded as a great evil in our land, and it desires the government, if it be possible, to devise some way by which this evil can be removed.[49]

Notwithstanding their obvious ambivalence concerning the question of slavery, Lutherans in the United States launched their second major organized outreach effort towards African Americans, free and slave, in 1817 with the passage of the so-called Five

Point Plan by the North Carolina Synod. By the onset of the Civil War, that is, within 44 years, African Americans constituted 10 to 20 percent of the membership of the Lutheran synods of the South. At no other time in the history of American Lutheranism have African Americans made up so large a proportion of the membership of the Lutheran church.

Immediately following the Civil War, American Lutherans adopted a new policy of working with black Americans. The Tennessee Synod was the first to articulate this new policy in 1866 when it urged African American Lutherans to form separate black congregations as well as a separate ecclesiastical organization. It based this recommendation on the grounds that "God has made (plainly marked distinctions) between us [whites] and them [blacks], giving different colors, and so forth."[50] The North and South Carolina Synods followed suit, passing almost identical resolutions. The 1866 policy decision marked the beginning of a policy of organizing African Americans into separate congregations in the Lutheran church.

That 1866 decision might have had merit as a mission strategy. There were, however, some deficiencies. First, the decision did not recognize the legitimacy of black culture, and therefore was not aimed at making Lutheranism an indigenous part of the African American community. Second, the call for a separate ecclesiastical organization would suggest that the policy was not ultimately aimed at bringing African Americans into full participation in the life of the Lutheran church. The Synodical Conference appears to have proceeded in much the same way in 1877 when it began its mission outreach to the black community. That practice continued until 1947 when the Synod adopted a policy of integrating black pastors into its districts.

B. Necessity of a Christian Response

We confront the issue of racism now because of the urgent need to assess where we are as individuals and as a church body committed to putting into practice our Christian faith. As individual Christians we must exercise constant vigilance in the face of persistent and devious efforts of Satan, who seeks to make an agony of our common life in this world and ultimately to separate us from the reconciling love of God. With utmost seriousness, we hear the apostles admonish us: "Put on the whole armor of God, that you may be able to stand against the wiles of the devil" (Eph. 6:11); "Be sober, be watchful. Your adversary the devil prowls around like a roaring lion, seeking some one to devour" (1 Peter 5:8). Have we been faithful, we must ask ourselves, as those baptized into Christ's death and resurrection, in drowning "by daily contrition and repentance" also this wretched work of our old Adam so that the new man may "daily emerge and arise to live before God in righteousness and purity forever"?[51]

As a church body The Lutheran Church—Missouri Synod has made numerous efforts over the years to deal with the evil of racism. Since 1956 the Synod has adopted resolutions, held conferences, and created new structures and policies aimed at addressing the problem in its midst.[52] The same can surely be said of numerous other church bodies. The question remains, however, whether such efforts have effectively isolated the real causes of racism and applied to them a biblical solution. To underline the necessity and the urgency of our present task, we consider the following.

1. The Changing Reality of Racism

Recent decades have witnessed significant changes in race relations in our society, as well as in the church in the United States. Many institutions have taken positive steps to include previously excluded groups. There also is social sensitivity at least to the terms "racism" and "prejudice." To avoid the stigmas that such labels bring, it has become increasingly important for the members of our society to maintain the self-image or self-perception of being nonprejudiced and nonracist.

It might be argued, however, that this change in self-consciousness has not been all for the good. It has served, at times, to camouflage what is a more subtle form of racism to which few have not at some point succumbed.[53] We have in mind here the well-intentioned person who genuinely professes egalitarianism or equal rights for all. He or she truly has the desire to reduce the consequences of racism. But there is present also a kind of ambivalence that we may call "aversion." Such a person experiences a conflict between negative feelings (which are not always conscious) toward African Americans, for example, and a conscience that seeks to repudiate or disassociate these feelings from a nonprejudiced self-image ("I'm not prejudiced, but . . ."). At the emotional level, the discomfort and uneasiness that often accompanies such aversion may lead to the avoidance of interracial contacts. And, a sense of superiority may develop, with the result that positive rather than negative characteristics are ascribed to oneself. For example, a person may not believe that African Americans are lazier than whites. He or she may simply suspect that whites are more ambitious than blacks.

No doubt many such proponents of egalitarianism, though internally ambivalent, have been among those responsible for the formulation and implementation of affirmative action programs. Critics point out that though well-meaning, these programs have often in fact undermined serious efforts at integration. The problem is that the focus of attention is frequently on the *consequences* of racism, not its causes. The consequences of racism are viewed as the causal agents in the continuing cycle of oppression. According to this way of thinking, the defect to be remedied is thought to reside within the victims of racism rather than within the persons and structures responsible for the defect in the first place.[54] Not surprisingly, programs are then devised to treat the victims of racism as the cause of their own victimization.[55]

2. The Problem of Integration

a. Integration and Black Ministry. A second reason for dealing with racism and its manifestations in church and society at this time is the issue of "integration." The Lutheran Church—Missouri Synod made concerted efforts to deal with this problem.[56] We may point to developments such as the following:

> 1877: The Evangelical Lutheran Synodical Conference, of which the Missouri Synod was a member, commissioned its first missionary to work among African Americans.[57]

> 1903: The Synodical Conference opened its first school, Immanuel Lutheran College and Seminary, to train African American church workers. Two other schools were subsequently opened to train African Americans for professional church work: Luther College (founded 1903 in New Orleans, Louisiana) and Selma Academy (founded 1922 in Selma, Alabama).[58]

> 1947: The Missouri Synod began the process of integrating the congregations and black pastors of the Synodical Conference into its various districts. In fact, The Lutheran Church—Missouri Synod officially adopted a policy of what is called "integration."[59]

> 1956: Subsequent to the 1954 United States Supreme Court ruling that "separate but equal" facilities for black persons in public schools do not meet the constitutional requirement for equal protection of the law, the Missouri Synod in 1956 resolved to follow a policy of integrated congregations.[60] Since 1956, the Synod has adopted numerous resolutions aimed at implementing the spirit of that resolution.

1961: The process of integrating the congregations and pastors of the Synodical Conference into the various districts of the Synod was completed.[61] In 1964 the United States Congress passed the Civil Rights Act, which was followed by other legislative acts and court decisions (e.g., Affirmative Action) to implement the 1954 Brown vs. Board of Education decision and the Civil Rights Act.

1977: The Synod organized the Commission on Black Ministry "to plan, to coordinate, and to expand black ministry" in its midst.[62]

This summary indicates that The Lutheran Church—Missouri Synod does indeed have a positive record in dealing with the question of integration and black ministry, and for this we thank God. At the same time, we need to consider a number of questions. First of all, the Synod's decision in 1947 to begin integrating black congregations and pastors into the districts of the Synod does not appear to have been motivated primarily by the desire to deal directly or decisively with the underlying problem of racism. Rather, that decision, which granted synodical membership to African American pastors and congregations, was made ostensibly and chiefly to prevent the imminent collapse of the Synodical Conference's administration of black ministry.[63] The Synodical Conference's approach to black ministry had given rise to a dilemma. As a result of the Conference's work for the growth of black ministry, an increasing number of black congregations had become, or were on the verge of becoming, self-supporting. However, black pastors and their congregations were not allowed to become members of the constituent synods of the Synodical Conference. Fundamental questions regarding the full inclusion of black brothers and sisters in Christ in the life and work of the church, including the basic problem of racism, remained unresolved.

A second stage of the Synod's policy of integration began in 1956 when it resolved that integration should take place within local congregations. No doubt the Synod was influenced by such factors as the 1954 Supreme Court decision abolishing the legal/moral basis for segregation and by the steady decline of inner-city white congregations (including the sale of property to non-Lutheran black churches).[64] Beginning in 1956, the Synod adopted a number of resolutions in response to growing interest in the issue of integration. Between 1975 and 1985 alone more than 56 resolutions concerning some aspect of integration were presented to the conventions of the Synod.[65] A cursory reading of these resolutions, however, reveals that integration as a means of carrying out God's mission among black people was not working as well as many in the Synod had hoped. In 1962 the Synod noted the "disturbing fact that [after nearly one hundred years] our membership gains among Negroes in the United States have been less than 17,000 when they should have been 229,000 if they had kept pace with our acquisition among the rest of the population."[66]

The Synod called attention to this fact again in 1981, when it underlined the need "To Open Every Ministry to Black Professional Church Workers" as a way of eliminating "the stigma of racism in the placement process of our church."[67] The Synod's hesitancy to proceed aggressively to this end is reflected, however, in the language of another resolution adopted in 1981. The Synod resolved that colleges and seminaries "be encouraged *to continue considering* employment of at least one Black faculty or professional staff member" (emphasis added).[68] This same hesitancy may well account for the disturbing fact that integration as a way of involving African Americans in synodical work at the managerial or executive level has not been working. The impression is given, therefore, that while the members of The Lutheran Church—Missouri Synod believe in integration, they have not practiced it effectively at the level of church-wide structure.[69]

b. Integration and Assimilation. The reason for the apparent failure of the Synod's longstanding policy of carrying out black ministry through integration may in turn be due in large part to a failure to give careful thought to precisely what integration means, not only theoretically but also practically. Little consideration seems to have been given to this matter.

Integration, as popularly understood, means "opening up the system, letting in those who desire to come in." A review of black ministry programs in the history of the Synod reveals, however, that integration has in fact been understood as "assimilation." These two activities have often been confused with one another. As a sociological phenomenon, assimilation refers to the disappearance of all former cultural differences so that the individual is no longer distinguishable from the group into which he or she has been assimilated. This, of course, cannot happen unless one is let "in." Integration, on the other hand, does not refer to the disappearance of differences so that the individual "integrated" becomes indistinguishable from the group (that, more appropriately, is called "cultural conversion"). Nor does integration entail primarily the removal of barriers that would hinder entry into the given group (that, more appropriately, is "desegregation"). Properly understood, integration denotes "the bringing of different racial or ethnic groups into free and equal association."[70] In practical terms, this means structural participation so there is equity with respect to "input" (institutional participation and decision making) and "outcome," that is, all those who participate in a given institution receive equivalent goods, services, and benefits.

Integration *as assimilation* is perceived by many among ethnic minorities, including especially African Americans, as a call for the surrender of one's heritage and identity in order not only to "get in," but also to become what others label as fully "human." This kind of assimilation into the church (as an institution that bears the Christian faith), therefore, strikes at the very heart of the African American identity and sense of selfhood, producing self-hatred, alienation, powerlessness, and dependency. The response of many is not to join "integrated" churches,[71] but to join those churches which unambiguously proclaim God's goodness and wisdom in his creation, his continuing sovereignty over his creation, his victory over every kind of sin (even the sin of racism) through the work of his Son, and his promises to empower them continually to live out Christ's victory and deliverance in this world and in the world to come. Such churches recognize and affirm the wonderful variety and diversity of the membership of the body of Christ, while at the same time rejoicing in its unity in Christ.

3. The Subtleties of Racism: Racial Disadvantage

Few today will fail to recognize conspicuous oppression and enslavement of racial groupings as blatantly racist. Often more difficult to recognize are the subtle and varied forms by which the heritage of racism continues to disadvantage members of minority groups. This is what we mean by "racial disadvantage."

By virtue of the historical realities of racism, racial minorities do not have the same legacy of advantage as do white Americans. Therefore, in our increasingly pluralistic and diverse society, to insist upon mere access to already existing institutions or to advance "equal opportunity" in those institutions may be only a way of perpetuating the disadvantage of a prior inequality. Racial disadvantage becomes increasingly intense and offensive if access to society's institutions demands conformity to ethnocentric norms unrelated to the common goods and services for which these institutions exist. We may cite, for example, the case of the California judge who prohibited the use of the Spanish language anywhere in the courthouse, not only in the performance of official duties, but during coffee breaks.[72]

Because racism is so much a part of the American worldview, it is often difficult for us to recognize it when we see it. We become insensitive to expressions of it. Many examples could be given, but consider something as simple as the language we use in our dealings with each other. Take the use of the word "qualified." To speak of someone as "qualified" to some may carry no racial overtones. To others it is a code word in the lexicon of derisive terms.

4. The Crisis of Self-Identity

Some anthropologists have argued that racism is one way in which individuals in modern western society have sought to answer the questions "Who am I?" or "What does it mean to be human?"[73] Suggesting that there are uniquely western answers to these questions, they hold that this response was prompted by the move out of ethnically homogeneous societies and by confrontation with the diversity of the human family. Furthermore, these anthropologists theorize that as human societies become more complex, the issue of what it means to be human is raised with increasing urgency. Ultimately, the most enduring answer is felt to be a religious one.[74] While racism is an extremely complex social phenomenon, the question of self-identity remains, both for perpetrator and victim, an ongoing problem of profound proportions.

5. Crimes of Racism

The crimes that have been committed in the name of racism will not, nor should they for various reasons, be forgotten.[75] We reject the notion that anyone should feel guilt-ridden for the crimes committed by one's forebears. But future generations must be ever mindful of the extremes to which sinful human beings will go when they yield to the lust for power coupled with the power of hatred, lest the horrors of the past be repeated. Racism has led to atrocities against native Americans in the 19th century, to the wholesale murder of the Holocaust in our lifetime in Europe, to the killing of hundreds of thousands of Armenian Christians after World War I, to the tragedies of South African apartheid, and most recently to the agonies of "ethnic cleansing" in the former Yugoslavia. The horrifying depths to which those taken captive by the evil of racism have fallen serve as a sobering reminder of the gravity of the problem we all face and to which only the church, entrusted with the message of God's reconciling Gospel, can bring ultimate resolution.

II. BIBLICAL PERSPECTIVE ON RACISM

Racism, as we have seen, is a *belief* system founded on the supposition that inherent, biological differences (or, in some cases, ethnic or cultural differences) among various human groups not only determine social or human achievement, but also the value of individual members of the human family. Those who adhere to its claims usually act as if their race is superior and therefore entitled to the right to rule over others. We do not hesitate at the outset to label racism and its supporting rationale as fundamentally incompatible with what the Scriptures teach concerning human beings and their relationship with God. However, the question before us is, what are the scriptural principles that lead us to make this judgment? It is to the theological issues raised by racism that we now turn, and we do so in light of what we have learned from the Scriptures to confess concerning the God who has created, redeemed, and sanctified us.

A. God Is the Creator of All Human Beings

Standing in the middle of the Areopagus in Athens the apostle Paul spoke of "the God who made the world and everything in it, being Lord of heaven and earth," declaring that this God is the one who "made from one every nation of men to live on all the face of the earth" (Acts 17:24, 26). The apostle here proclaims that God created out of one man all members of the human family, established their allotted place in human history, and desires that they all seek him (Acts 17:27). Against all claims to racial or ethnic superiority, the apostle unambiguously affirms the unity of humankind. Without differentiation, all of humanity owes its origin to God's creative act. Fitting also on earth, therefore, is the celestial hymn of the twenty-four elders in Revelation 4: "Worthy art thou, our Lord and God, to receive glory and honor and power for thou didst create all things, and by thy will they existed and were created" (Rev. 4:11).

Racist lines of demarcation between human beings declaring some to be lesser members of humankind are, therefore, a blasphemous affront to our Creator. Likewise, any affirmations of superiority or comparative worth that are based on differences in the nature of persons as human beings are to be regarded as an indictment of God's work as Creator.

B. The Dignity of All Human Beings Is Given by God, Not Achieved or Earned

Our God, "who created the heavens and stretched them out, who spread forth the earth and what comes from it," is the God "who gives breath to the people upon it and spirit to those who walk in it" (Is. 42:5). Not even the tragic fall of humankind into sin has erased the central biblical affirmation, so eloquently summarized by Luther, that "God has made me and all creatures." "To the Lord your God," Moses wrote to those upon whom the Lord has set his heart in love, "belong heaven and the heavens of heavens, the earth with all that is in it" (Deut. 10:14). In repentance the people need to remember that "the Lord your God is God of gods and Lord of lords, the great, the mighty, and terrible

God, *who is not partial* and takes no bribe" (Deut. 10:17; emphasis added). *No* human being, however distinguishable from a human standpoint, is any less fully God's creature—created in his image (Gen. 1:26–27; 9:6; cf. Acts 17:25, 26).

No less central to the biblical doctrine of creation is the truth that the value of all human beings is grounded ultimately in the value God places upon them. The value of a person is not determined by observable degrees of relative worth. Instead, it is bestowed in love by him who, the psalmist thankfully acknowledges, "didst form my inward parts" and who "knit me together in my mother's womb" (Ps. 139:13). Contemplating the miracle of his own creation, the psalmist is moved to declare, "I praise thee for thou art fearful and wonderful. Wonderful are thy works!" (Ps. 139:14).

In racist ideology the worth or value of an individual or group is determined principally, if not solely, by genetic origin and/or biological characteristics. Race, biologically defined, becomes the basis for drawing conclusions concerning aptitudes, abilities, and personality characteristics of individuals, for the purpose, in turn, of making a statement about the comparative worth of a person as a human being. Ironically, the twisted logic of racism makes use of biology to wrest from God the means by which he continues his creative work.

C. God Created All Human Beings to Honor and Serve Him Alone

When God created Adam, he made a creature who would live in a unique relationship with himself (Gen. 1:26–28; 2:15–17). Unlike the rest of all creation, Adam and Eve were created to worship and serve God in a most personal, intimate way. To be sure, to live *under* their Creator in obedience to the Word, and in utter dependence upon him, meant at the same time that they were to live *over* the rest of creation. But Adam and Eve were not autonomous beings. They were to rule over creation in God's behalf but with accountability to him (Gen. 1:26, 28). And they were to place their trust in God alone and to serve him alone (Deut. 10:12, 20).

When Adam and Eve disobeyed God in the garden they succumbed to the temptation to be "like God" (Gen. 3:5), God's rival. This is the sin of pride: the deification of self and the rejection of one's relationship to God as creature to Creator. In their solidarity with Adam, all who are born into the human family joined in Adam's sin (Rom. 5:12). The grave consequence of humankind's rebellion against God is that Adam's progeny worship and serve "the creature rather than the Creator, who is blessed for ever! Amen" (Rom. 1:25). The effects of this root sin of idolatry are tragic also for the relationship of human beings to one another. Indeed, "Idolatry opens the floodgates for vices which destroy society and turn creation back into terrible chaos. In this way the curse of God's wrath accomplishes its purpose."[76]

"That to which your heart clings and entrusts itself is, I say, really your God," Martin Luther wrote in the Large Catechism on the First Commandment, "You shall have no other gods."[77] By definition, racism grounds the identity and security of human life in self rather than God, in creature rather than the Creator, apart from whom a human being *has* no identity or security. Self-indulgent pride in "race," therefore, must be regarded as idolatry in one of its crassest forms. It is an attempt to be "like God."

D. In Jesus Christ God Became a Man and So Identified Himself Fully with Every Member of the Human Family

Of Jesus Christ the apostle John wrote, "And the Word became flesh and dwelt among us, full of grace and truth; we

have beheld his glory, glory as of the only Son from the Father"
(John 1:14). He was "descended from David according to the flesh
and designated Son of God in power according to the Spirit of
holiness by his resurrection from the dead" (Rom. 1:3). He was
"made like his brethren in every respect" except for sin (Heb.
2:17; cf. 4:15; 5:2). The genealogies of Jesus reveal that he is bound
by ties of kinship not only to Israel but to all of humanity and
that his mission embraces all of humankind (Matt. 1:1–17; Luke
3:23–38).[78]

Any claim that there is something about the nature of
another human being as such that renders that person to be of
inferior value not only denies the biblical doctrine of creation,
but also calls into question what the Scriptures teach about the
incarnation of Jesus Christ, the Son of God. As a human, Jesus
descended from Adam, whom God created (Luke 3:38), and whom
all human beings have as progenitor. To deny the full humanity
of any fellow human being is at the same time to compromise
the apostolic truth that in Christ "the whole fullness of deity
dwells *bodily*" (σωματικός, Col. 2:9), that is, that he truly "was
made man" (Nicene Creed).

Christians of differing national or ethnic origins must also
be wary of the temptation to claim Christ as *exclusively* their own,
as if to say that their view of him most closely approximates the
biblical portrayal of him.[79]

E. God Sent His Son Jesus Christ to Be the Savior of All Human Beings, in Whatever Nation or Culture They May Be Found

God our Savior, St. Paul wrote to Timothy, "desires all
men to be saved and to come to the knowledge of the truth.
For there is one God, and there is one mediator between God
and men, the man Christ Jesus, who gave himself as a ran-
som for all" (1 Tim. 2:3–6). "In Christ," he writes also to the

Corinthians, "God was reconciling the world to himself, not counting their trespasses against them" (2 Cor. 5:19). In obedience to Christ's command to make disciples of all nations, the apostles proclaimed the Gospel to Jew and Gentile alike. Peter learned from the vision in Simon's house, with specific reference to the Gentile Cornelius in Caesarea, that "God shows no partiality, but in every nation any one who fears him and does what is right is acceptable to him" (Acts 10:34–35). In response to the questions "Is God the God of Jews only? Is he not the God of Gentiles also?" St. Paul does not hesitate to answer, "Yes, of the Gentiles also, since God is one" (Rom. 3:29–30). Again and again in the apocalyptic vision of St. John, we read that God in Jesus Christ has completed his work of salvation for and in all kindreds, peoples, languages, and nations (Rev. 5:8–9; 7:9, 10; 11:9; 13:7; 14:6; 17:15).

Racism as "the ideological doctrine of a providential selection and election of human races"[80] stands in diametrical opposition to the Gospel of God revealed in the Scriptures, according to which God has acquired the forgiveness of sins for *all* people by declaring that the world for Christ's sake has been forgiven. God's love for the world is indiscriminate and embraces people of all cultures. In its more subtle form, racism may also manifest itself in the limited focus of Christian mission activities, undermining Christ's mandate to "Go therefore and make disciples of all nations, baptizing them in the name of the Father and of the Son and of the Holy Spirit" (Matt. 28:19). Biological homogeneity and/or cultural uniformity—often more implicitly than explicitly—become a justifying rationale for not proclaiming the Gospel to certain individuals and groups, or at least not proclaiming it with equal fervor. The scope of God's redemptive work is narrowed, a stumbling block is placed in the way of its free and full proclamation, and the work of God's Spirit is quenched (1 Thess. 5:19).

F. Jesus Christ Has Removed All Barriers That Stand between Human Beings, Making Peace through His Cross

As the Gospel was being proclaimed in the ancient world, the apostles had to deal with the historic wall of separation that existed between Jews and Gentiles.[81] The apostles' solution to this problem was not the removal of differences, but the proclamation of the Gospel of Jesus Christ who through his work on the cross made Christians one. St. Paul wrote to the Ephesians, "But now in Christ Jesus you who once were far off have been brought near in the blood of Christ. For he is our peace, who has made us both one, and has broken down the dividing wall of hostility, by abolishing in his flesh the law of commandments and ordinances, that he might create in himself one new man in place of two, so making peace, and might reconcile us both to God in one body through the cross, thereby bringing the hostility to an end" (Eph. 2:13–16). Those who were once segregated in hostility, have now been united with one another and with God. They are bound together in a baptismal unity that transcends all differences of race, social status, or sex that divide human beings.[82]

Racism in the church poisons and cripples all sincere efforts "to maintain the unity of the Spirit in the bond of peace" (Eph. 4:3). Physical characteristics or cultural customs are made to serve as "a dividing wall of hostility" that separates brothers and sisters in Christ—to which the only appropriate response must be "Is Christ divided?" (1 Cor. 1:13). Racism in the church, in its essence, is a blatant denial of the unity of the body of Christ, into which all who have been baptized into his name have been incorporated: "For by one Spirit we were all baptized into one body—Jews or Greeks, slaves or free—and all were made to drink of one Spirit" (1 Cor. 12:13). "There is one body and one Spirit, just as you were called to the one hope that belongs to your call, one Lord, one faith, one baptism, one God and Father of us all, who is above all and through all and in all" (Eph. 4:4–6). This unity, it should be emphasized, *transcends* differences among human beings. It does not call for the elimination of those differences. Moreover, when those who participate in the Lord's Supper do so unrepentant of the sin of racism, they "despise the church of God" (1 Cor. 11:22). "The cup of blessing which we bless," asks Paul, "is it not a participation in the blood of Christ? The bread which we break, is it not a participation in the body of Christ? Because there is one bread, we who are many are one body, for we all partake of the one bread" (1 Cor. 10:16–17). What better way to receive forgiveness also for the sin of racism than through this sacrament which unites us with our brothers and sisters in Christ, even those whom we may be tempted to "despise" as inferior.

G. Love Produced in Christians by the Holy Spirit Embraces, without Distinction, All People in Their Need

Foremost in the list of "the fruit of the Spirit," which is to characterize the life of those who have been set free from the tyranny of their sinful flesh, is love (Gal. 5:22; cf. 5:13–26). The "new commandment" given by Jesus to his disciples is that they love one another as he has loved them, for "by this all men will know that you are my disciples, if you have love for one another" (John 13:35; cf. 1 John 2:8–11; 4:20–5:3; Phil. 2: 4–5). The Savior wills that those whom he has loved also become the bearers of his love to his whole creation. He requires his disciples to love all those whom they encounter in life. A distinguishing feature of the love he creates by his Spirit in the lives of his people is its nondiscriminatory character. Just as "God so loved the world that he gave his only Son," so now those who live by faith in God's Son are to live in love for all people. "If anyone says, 'I love God,'" says John, "and hates his brother, he is a liar; for he who does not love his brother whom he has seen, cannot love

God whom he has not seen. And this commandment we have from him, that he who loves God should love his brother also" (1 John 4:20–21).

Employing a logic similar to that countered by James in the second chapter of his letter, some may argue that the command to love one's neighbor carries with it the freedom to love one particular neighbor of one's choice. The apostle's response to this way of reasoning is that such self-indulgent use of the divine mandate to love one's neighbor is sin. The law of love cannot be made an excuse for respect of persons. That is to say, keeping one precept of the law does not give one license to disobey the full requirements of the law of love. James says, "If you really fulfill the royal law, according to the scripture, 'You shall love your neighbor as yourself,' you do well. But if you show partiality, you commit sin, and are convicted by the law as transgressors" (James 2:8–9).

Love for our neighbor requires that we defend him or her against wrong (Prov. 31:8–9) and pursue those things that are just and fair. As the Decalogue had already made clear, and as the Old Testament prophets unceasingly reminded the people, the worship of the Lord (Yahweh) entails a respect for the rights of others (e.g., Ex. 20:12–17; Amos 5:14–15; Is. 1:10–17; Micah 6:6–8). Such regard for the rights of the neighbor is reflected in Old Testament legislation designed to help especially those who are in danger of being victims of injustice and oppression, e.g., widows, orphans, and foreigners (Ex. 22:21–24; Lev. 19:33–34; Deut. 24:14–15; Is. 10:1–4; Jer. 7:5–7; 9:23–24; 21:12; 22:3; Zech. 7:9–10). God is a God of justice, and it is not his will that human beings exploit others. The welfare of one's neighbor also requires that in the civil realm Christian citizens work to extend justice to others by advocating the passage of just laws, the rescinding of unjust laws, and the responsible enforcement of all law (Rom. 13:1–7; 1 Peter 2:13–17).

Racism's insensitivity to the plight of those suffering wrong, its readiness to relieve itself from the responsibility to help those in need, and its callousness in the face of the biblical mandate to "honor all men" (1 Peter 2:17) must be resolutely and vigorously resisted if the church is to be faithful to the apostolic command to "do good to all men, and especially to those who are of the household of faith" (Gal. 6:10). Such resistance is possible only through the power of God's Spirit working through Word and sacraments, leading sinners to true repentance and to faith in Christ's forgiveness, and filling them with the all-embracing love of their Savior.

H. Through the Means of Grace the Holy Spirit Works within the Context of All Cultures to Bring People to Faith in Jesus Christ and to Move Them to Worship Him

No one particular group is the best or more effective medium through which God can communicate to his creatures. God is not bound by, nor is he dependent on, one group or the other to make effective the Gospel and the sacraments. Rather, he enters his creation and communicates with human beings in terms that are comprehensible to them in their differences. The day of Pentecost demonstrates this dramatically. The apostles proclaimed the Word of God to people "from every nation under heaven." Each person present "heard them speaking in his own language" (Acts 2:5–6).

At the same time, the Spirit of God moves those who believe the Gospel to worship their Lord in culturally divergent forms.[83] Touching on this point is the discourse of Jesus with the Samaritan woman at the well. The issue raised by the woman of Samaria was whether proper worship takes place on Mt. Gerizim or in Jerusalem. To this Jesus responded, "neither on this mountain nor in Jerusalem will you worship the Father . . . true worshippers will worship the Father in spirit and truth, for such the Father seeks to worship him. God is spirit, and those who worship him must worship in spirit and truth" (John 4:21–24). In the new covenant, true worship is not tied to the place or cultic tradition of either Gerizim or Jerusalem, however important such tradition may be for each. True worship takes place where, through the Gospel and sacraments ("as through means"), God "gives the Holy Spirit, who works faith, when and where he pleases, in those who hear the Gospel" (AC V, 2).

The Lutheran confessors emphasized that "it is sufficient for the true unity of the Christian church that the Gospel be preached in conformity with a pure understanding of it and that the sacraments be administered in accordance with the divine Word. It is not necessary for the true unity of the Christian church that ceremonies, instituted by men, should be observed uniformly in all places" (AC VII, 2–3). The Scriptures permit us readily to affirm particular cultural and ethnic expressions in Christian worship. Deeply problematic, however, is any claim that one particular culturally shaped response to God's goodness and grace is in and of itself superior to others.[84] God's work through the means of grace is effective in or through many and varied cultural forms, through which God is properly worshipped.

l. Through the Means of Grace God Empowers Christians "to Abstain from the Passions of the Flesh That Wage War against the Soul," Including the Sin of Racism

The living and abiding Word of God, the Gospel, makes us new creatures through the Holy Spirit, enabling us to discard the sins of the unregenerate life (1 Peter 1:12, 22–23; 2:1–3). As the new birth in which God binds us to Christ's death to sin and imparts to us the new life of the Holy Spirit, Holy Baptism places us into the way of Jesus, whose free love was for all persons and toward all persons. Baptism, therefore, frees us from all sins that characterize life apart from God. Just as speaking evil of others, quarreling, malice, and hatred toward others was far from the mind of Christ, so too the minds of those regenerated in Baptism are to be free from such evils. Likewise, as the body of Christ broken for the forgiveness of sin and as the blood of Christ shed for the many, the Lord's Supper unites us to the full and complete humanity of him who is the Creator of all and the Savior of all.

The struggle against the sin of racism and the sins it entails is a continual striving to be conformed to the Lord Jesus in a spiritual war that seriously threatens to erode faith and to disparage the witness of the church to the Gospel of her Lord. Therefore, we Christians must not underestimate the evil of racism in the human heart, but we are to return daily in repentance to the Christ who loves us, so that also in this matter the victory of Christ's own grace and love may be manifested in our personal lives.

Significantly, the "catalogs" of vices that we find in the New Testament list especially those sins that are destructive of human relationships (see e.g., Rom. 1:28–32; Gal. 5:19–21; Col. 3:5–9). While not mentioned expressly as such, racism belongs in this category of the sins of the flesh, for it is in its very nature divisive of human associations not only in the fellowship of Christ's church but in society in general. Against this sin also, then, St. Paul exhorts us to "stand therefore, having girded your loins with truth, and having put on the breastplate of righteousness, and having shod your feet with the equipment of the gospel of peace . . . And take the helmet of salvation, and the sword of the Spirit, which is the word of God" (Eph. 6:14–17).

III. COMBATTING RACISM IN THE CHURCH

In the first two sections of this study, we have discussed what racism is and why the church needs to address the problem at this time. We have also focused on the scriptural truths that speak to the issue. In this last section, we shall do two things: (1) describe some of the barriers Christians face and will have to overcome as they confront racism in their midst; (2) outline some guiding principles for combatting and overcoming racism in the church and in the community.

A. Barriers to Overcoming Racism

As we Christians—who are at the same time saints and sinners—confront the sin of racism, we must first of all realize that we will have to overcome a host of obstacles that are constantly being erected by the world, the devil, and our own sinful flesh. A first and crucial step in tackling the problem of racism is the identification and removal of these barriers. We call attention, therefore, to the following hindrances to overcoming racism, recognizing that this is, of course, not an exhaustive list.

1. Denial

By "denial" we mean the refusal to confront a problem by denying that it exists. No matter what form it takes, denial is an age-old strategy that Satan uses to blind people to the reality of their sins and thereby to hold them in bondage. Since denial involves a refusal to recognize, confess, and repent of sin, it is a matter of grave spiritual consequence. When we deny sin, God cannot enter with his forgiveness and with his healing power. We, not someone else, then become the victims of our own self-deception (1 John 1:8). However, with the exhortation to confess sin comes the promise that our heavenly Father "will forgive our sins and cleanse us from all unrighteousness" (1 John 1:9). As often as we confess our sins, we claim God's promise to wash us and make us as "white as snow" (Is. 1:18) in the life-giving waters of our Baptism. For this reason we also approach Christ's table frequently and eagerly to receive his true body and blood, "Given and shed for you for the forgiveness of sins," so that we might be strengthened in faith and holy living.

2. Untenable Assumptions

The first untenable assumption that frustrates attempts to deal with racism in the church is what some have called the "good will assumption." This is the popular belief that "all Christians" (i.e., people of "good will") will automatically recognize that racism is morally wrong and that they will therefore spontaneously do the right thing. Thus, the church (so the thinking goes) need not concern itself with this issue. However, the biblical depiction of the total depravity of sinful human beings and of the effects of sin in our life makes it clear that members of the church also can be guilty of something as deplorable as racism (both by sins of commission and of omission). Only the continuous application of Law and Gospel will diagnose and cure the problem.

Related to this is a second assumption that the preaching of Law and Gospel merely in some abstract, detached sense—without careful and specific applications of the way the sin of racism actually works in the lives of people—will root out the sin. Lutheran pastors may well be surprised to discover that their devout members are carrying burdens of racism that they as pastors have been addressing for years. Pastors may often be too shy about speaking concretely to what racism is and what it does to people. Therefore, people may hear but not really understand how God's Law—as well as his Gospel—applies to them personally and specifically when it comes to the sin of racism.

A third assumption that frequently impedes efforts to identify and remove racism is the notion that solving this problem is a short-term process. If our description of the nature of racism in its many and changing forms has merit, then we can be certain that there is no "quick fix" to this problem. Improvement will come about only by repeated exposure to its sinfulness and calls to repentance, followed by Christ's sure and clear word of absolution, which alone has the power to change hearts and lives. Careful instruction will also need to be given concerning how such racist attitudes are passed along to the next generation, and how patterns of behavior at church, at home, at work, and at school (i.e., in all life situations) may be broken. In the early Christian church, it took a long time before the attitude of Jewish Christians toward Gentiles and patterns of interaction between these two groups began to change (Gal. 2:14). But by God's grace and the Spirit's power, change did—and still can—occur.

A fourth untenable assumption is that racism in the church will be solved by "education," that is, merely by imparting the "right facts" to people. As necessary and helpful as this approach is, it will not eradicate racism by itself. The sin of racism is not merely a matter of the intellect. The intellect itself is blinded by the power of sin and is set in opposition to God's will concerning attitudes toward others (Eph. 4:18–19). To be sure, the intense spiritual struggle involved in combatting racism requires laying out and applying the facts. But these facts and their application do not themselves change the attitudes and behavior of people. What is required, once again, is the wise, discerning application of the living and active Word of God, which is "sharper than any two-edged sword, piercing to the division of soul and spirit, of joints and marrow, and discerning the thoughts and intentions of the heart" (Heb. 4:12). Once God's Law has done its work, our hearts can then be "sprinkled clean from an evil conscience" (Heb. 10:22) by the Gospel and our new nature "renewed in knowledge after the image of its creator" (Col. 3:10).

3. Paternalism

"Paternalism" is the claim or attempt to supply the needs or to regulate the lives of others, like a father does in the case of his children. Paternalism grows out of attitudes of self-importance and is frequently rationalized as an expression of Christian concern. To the detriment of healthy intergroup relations, however, paternalism tends to trivialize minority group persons, portraying them as incapable of caring for themselves or functioning responsibly. The opposite of paternalism is the assumption by members of a minority group that *all* members of the majority group will always patronize them and subject them to paternalistic patterns of behavior. Paternalism and its opposite are often built into the ethos and language of both majority and minority group cultures. Only when dealt with honestly and openly in the common recognition that there is but "one God and Father of us all, who is above all and through all and in all" (Eph. 4:6), can such mindsets be changed and this barrier overcome.

4. Different Meanings and Frames of Reference

When majority and minority groups come together to discuss the issue of racism, they frequently use the same terms, but assign completely different meanings to them (e.g., "qualified," "minority"). Unless carefully planned and executed, such discussions only serve to confirm preexisting suspicions and tensions. This barrier, however, can be transformed into an avenue to further understanding. Since different meanings given to the same terms are based on varying life experiences, and because not all groups will have the same experiences, conversation aimed at increased understanding between people in this area can do much to remove the walls that exist. It is also important that when Christians work together to resolve these differences they be careful to avoid giving offense by their imprecise speech, and that they be careful not to take offense where none is intended (Rom. 12:14, 17; 14:5, 13).

5. Fear of Differences

The fear of racial and cultural differences can be strongly counterproductive in human relationships. Within the church, ethnic caucuses, for example, can be met with concern about what "they" really want, the fear that "they" will cause divisions and disunity in the church, or that "they" want to "take over" in the church.

But ethnic differences need not be divisive. It has been observed that "ethnicity is far from being a divisive force in society. It can be viewed as a constructive (if not) . . . an inevitable one." While it is true that "diversity may lead to misery in the world," it is also true that without the ability to find a place for themselves in the midst of diversity, people "may not be able to cope with the world at all."[85] Christians above all are in a position to recognize that "the body does not consist of one member but of many," and that "if one member suffers, all suffer together; if one member is honored, all rejoice together" (1 Cor. 12:14, 26).

6. Fear of Change

The dismantling of racism will necessarily bring marked changes in attitudes, actions, relationships, and structures. However, many people feel threatened by the prospect of change of any kind. The fear of such change may immobilize some and lead others to fight desperately, perhaps even irrationally, to maintain the status quo. The church must constantly work to assist its members in evaluating and accepting change properly, not on the basis of personal "likes" and "dislikes," but according to God's will and in keeping with his mission that the church faithfully proclaim the Gospel of his Son to all people. Making everything work *for* this mission, and not against it, is a compelling reason for change. And, we keep in mind that the Gospel we proclaim to others is the same Gospel we claim for ourselves—the good news that saves us, sets us free, and strengthens us for service to Christ.

B. Guiding Principles

The following principles are commended to the church for guidance in responding to the evils of racism. They are purposely designed to be general in nature. This is because we do not believe that it is possible to anticipate specifically what actions might result from the application of these principles to the various causes and consequences of racism that presently confront the church and hinder the full proclamation of the Gospel. As we reflect on these principles we need to emphasize once again that it is this Gospel alone, not our human efforts, that provides us as Christians with the power to deal with racism.

1. The unity of the body of Christ is to be reflected in the church's structure, life, and work.

On the night before his crucifixion, Jesus prayed for his disciples "that they may all be one; even as thou, Father, art in me, and I in thee, that they also may be in us, so that the world may believe that thou hast sent me" (John 17:21). St. Paul wrote, "For just as the body is one and has many members, and all the members of the body, though many, are one body, so it is with Christ. For by one Spirit we were all baptized into one body— Jews or Greeks, slaves or free—and all were made to drink of one Spirit" (1 Cor. 12:12–13).

The implication of this principle, based on Scripture passages such as those cited above, is unmistakably clear: the unity of the church transcends every race and culture and is to be manifested in the full acceptance and inclusion of all peoples. There is no "Anglo-Caucasian," no "African-American," no "Hispanic-American," no "Vietnamese-American," or other "hyphenated" citizen in the sight of God, as if to imply that some are more worthy than others to join the company of those who call on his name. We must quickly add that to affirm a particular race and culture does not imply separatism. Rather, such affirmation is a way of identifying those persons whom the Lord has given to his church, together with their special gifts, for the benefit of all.

2. The Scriptures require that the church confront moral evil in its midst, including the sin of racism.

Reminding the Ephesian Christians to "take no part in the unfruitful works of darkness, but instead expose them," St. Paul continues by exhorting them to "look carefully then how you walk, not as unwise men but as wise, making the most of the time, because the days are evil. Therefore, do not be foolish, but understand what the will of the Lord is" (Eph. 5:11, 15–17). Racism must be regarded among the "works of darkness" that produce nothing of any value to anyone. The church, aware of its history in the United States, must continually employ methods—grounded in the Word and sacraments and in the proper distinction between Law and Gospel—to expose, condemn, and remove it. Not to do so is to participate in perpetuating institutional and cultural racism and to hinder effective and God-pleasing outreach with the Gospel.

3. The church will commit itself to respond to racism in both word and deed by showing love and respect to all for whom Christ died.

Honor and esteem for all people will be reflected in the church's public witness to the Gospel of Jesus Christ (1 Peter

2:17; Gal. 6:10; 2 Cor. 6:3). The community of the baptized will make it known that it seeks to be enriched by all God-pleasing differences. By accepting all people as the objects of God's inestimable love, believers make known God's way of countering racism. God's love, which has equally saved, forgiven, accepted, and blessed all his children, will cause his people to commit themselves to love and to respect other human beings equally, and to do so in deeds, not only with pious-sounding resolutions and good intentions.

4. When a Christian congregation finds itself in a changing or changed community, it will reach out to the newcomers and genuinely welcome them to become members of the Christian family.

One of the more obvious consequences of racism in the history of Christian churches in our country is "white Anglo-Caucasian flight" from neighborhoods and communities in ethnic transition. The Lutheran Church—Missouri Synod has not been an exception. It has been a source of great sadness to witness the relocation of large urban congregations of the Synod to suburban areas, with the subsequent sale of their urban facilities to other church bodies, and often with little or no thought given to providing for witness to the new entrants to the community. And, such relocation is due to what some are even bold to say publicly without shame, "*they* are moving into our neighborhood."

Christian congregations need to be ready to serve new entrants to their community as soon as they arrive, and not after most of the former members of the congregation have already fled. Concern ought not merely be to "save the congregation." Survival of the congregation as an institution is not an acceptable reason for Christian outreach. The opportunity to share Christ with as many people as possible, celebrating diversity and fostering unity by the power of God's Spirit, is the finest expression of Christian identity and purpose.

5. When a Christian congregation includes new members of differing backgrounds, it will do all in its power to create a healthy climate for them in order to make them feel that they are truly welcome as members of that family.

There is no room in the body of Christ for the establishment of a "we/they" dichotomy. Such a mindset brings to light the sad truth that if the congregation had a preference, it would never choose to have these folks, so different from the rest, in the same religious organization. Merely to tolerate anyone, however, is another expression of exclusion.

What attracts and convinces new entrants to a community is the eagerness of a Christian congregation to welcome them and to "give themselves away" to the newcomers. They are drawn to congregations that encourage them in every demonstrable way to assume all the rights and privileges of their membership and to "take over" as part of the new generation of believers. An attitude such as this will lead to the kind of harmony God wills for his church, and will keep the congregation from becoming entrapped in patterns of assimilation that promote and perpetuate racism in the church rather than remove it.

When a congregation under the guidance of the Holy Spirit genuinely welcomes new members, changes will take place. These changes will reflect the full range of cultures represented in the Christian family. Openness to change in such things as the order of worship, the hymnody, the expressions of love and friendship, as well as the recreational life of the congregation, will reveal the congregation's eagerness to embrace all people in the love of Christ. Changes grounded in the truth of God's Word and motivated by love for his people will enhance every aspect of the life and work of the congregation.

6. In its new expression of life together, the Christian congregation will through the power of God's Word encourage all of its members to exercise their responsibilities and prerogatives of Christian service.

The Christian congregation will actively involve the various groupings in its midst when it comes to decision-making, service on boards and committees, preparation for ministry in the church, representation of the congregation at the district and synodical level, employment in the congregation, or any other aspect of the life and work of the congregation or church-at-large. It will operate on the basis of the insight revealed to St. Peter, "Truly I perceive that God shows no partiality" (Acts 10:34), not only in the granting of salvation but also in the full bestowal of the gifts of the Spirit (Acts 10:44–48).

7. When the church decides to share the Gospel in a community which is made up of a racial or ethnic group different from the majority of the members of the church, its goal and firm commitment will be to carry out the ministry of Word and sacrament by making use of the cultural forms of that community.

When the church decides to bring the Gospel to any community, it must "translate" the Gospel into the idiom of that community. The process of "translating" the Gospel into the idiom of the community (racial or ethnic) means articulating it in the cultural forms of that community so that the people can understand and respond to what is said. (This is sometimes referred to as "indigenization.") This way of proceeding is very much in keeping with St. Paul's missionary principle, "I have become all things to all men, that I might by all means save some" (1 Cor. 9:22). As people "hear" the truth of the Gospel in the context of their lives they are led by the Spirit of God to believe in and worship Christ.[86]

Indigenization occurs when the church shares the Gospel by working "inside" a particular community's culture (e.g., using its language, art, and music). The entire lifestyle there, including the worship of the congregation, will strive to be biblically and confessionally Lutheran, while at the same time being a true expression of that group's specific culture. These are in no way mutually exclusive.

All cultures, of course, contain structures and practices that are evil. The church must challenge all those aspects of culture that express the demonic and dehumanizing forces of evil, while affirming and celebrating the positive values of that culture.

The Lutheran reformers were classic examples of people who practiced indigenization with respect to the Gospel ministry. They did not define their task in ways that allowed for the abandonment of the historic and biblical Christian experience, or the creation of a new version of the "faith of the fathers." On the contrary, they insisted on the primacy of Scripture and the centrality of the sacraments in the life and work of the church. They sought to unite themselves with the historic community of faith, with its creeds and confessions, and to preserve those scriptural practices and worship forms Christians had developed over the centuries. All of this was done "inside" the culture of the people they sought to serve.

8. The church will regard those groups it hopes to serve not as "objects" of its ministry but as those whom our Lord calls to be "full partners" in the Gospel.

All people who are baptized into the Christian faith receive their life from Christ himself. "To be baptized in God's name is to be baptized not by men but by God himself."[87] They receive this gift through the ministry of others. They have also been called to a life of service to others, since our Lord has called us all to a life of service to others (John 13:15; Phil. 2:4–11). However, great sensitivity must be exercised so that certain people and/or groups are not categorized as people to be continuously "acted upon" by others in a way that implies that they are a second-class members of the kingdom of God. Similarly, when we approach members of "minority" or "majority" groups with the Gospel of Christ, we must view them as people who are being called to full participation in the life and mission of the institutional church at all levels—local, national, and international.

9. As the church responds to the Lord's mandate to "make disciples of all nations" in our time, it will recognize the special challenge of the core city as it confronts the problems of racism.

In our time, the cities of the world continue to be of critical importance for God's mission. The cities of contemporary America, in particular, are centers for the gathering of peoples from every nation. As in the ancient world, they are cultural centers where questions concerning the identity and meaning of human life are intense and receive their severest test, thus making them fertile ground for new religions. Our cities, especially our inner cities, reverberate with the cry for healing and peace, needs that only the Gospel can satisfy. With its myriad challenges and unprecedented opportunities, the peoples of the city must not be abandoned by the church or deemed less worthy of its attention due to factors arising from the problem of racism.

10. Given the complexity of life in the city and the enormity of the missionary task, pastors and congregations will work in concert with, not in opposition to, Christians of other church bodies.

In contemporary urban centers it is in many instances not possible for individual believers or congregations to carry out their mission to proclaim the Gospel to all in isolation from the rest of the community. Pastors and their congregations should be encouraged, therefore, to discover ways to cooperate with other Christians and members of the local community in programs or projects that confront racism and other community problems—e.g., drugs, hunger, homelessness, teenage pregnancies, and gangs. Such cooperative activity has a long history in many ethnic communities and can be carried out by members of The Lutheran Church—Missouri Synod in ways that are fully consistent with the Synod's traditional understanding of inter-Christian relationships.[88]

IV. CONCLUSION

We in The Lutheran Church—Missouri Synod have before us a wonderful opportunity to commit ourselves to strive toward making racism a thing of the past, and to demonstrate before a watching world how people of all cultures and groups can become one in Christ, who has made of many one body for the edification of all. Racism is sin. To the extent that racism continues to exist within the church the world is defining the purpose of God's creation. But those whom God has created, redeemed, and sanctified are to have fellowship with him and with each other, and to serve him and their fellow human beings. In Ephesians 2 St. Paul is unmistakably clear on this matter. In Christ God has destroyed all barriers between himself and human beings, as well as all barriers between human beings. As the apostle puts it, Jesus Christ came "that he might create in himself one new man in place of the two, so making peace" (2:15).

If the church is to proclaim the Gospel of Jesus Christ effectively to a world that is becoming smaller and smaller and at the same time being violently torn apart by racial and ethnic differences, the church itself will do well to pay heed to the counsel of St. James, who said, "But be doers of the word, and not hearers only, deceiving yourselves," and "show me your faith apart from your works, and I by my works will show you my faith" (James 1:22; 2:18).[89]

We now stand at the threshold of the 21st century. It is time to let our light shine and, through the proclamation of the glorious Gospel of our blessed God, to lead the way to the inclusion of all our sisters and brothers in Christ in the full exercise of the rights and privileges that belong to them as priests. What a beautiful opportunity we have to let God's will be done on earth as it most certainly is done in heaven, where there is not now, nor will there ever be, any partiality shown to anyone. We must all continually seek God's help in helping each other in our Synod to resist the temptations toward racist thinking and to eradicate its poisonous effects in our lives, that we may walk together in true unity of mind, heart, and purpose, even as we are one in Christ.

So if there is any encouragement in Christ, any
incentive of love, any participation in the Spirit, any
affection and sympathy, complete my joy by being of
the same mind, having the same love, being in full
accord and of one mind. Phil. 2:1–2

NOTES

Chapter One: General Introduction: My Story

1. See the following for a description of this history in the Reformed and Presbyterian tradition: Joel Alvis, *Religion and Race: Southern Presbyterians, 1946–1983* (Tuscaloosa, AL: University of Alabama Press, 1994); Peter Slade, *Open Friendship in a Closed Society: Mission, Mississippi, and a Theology of Friendship* (Oxford: Oxford University Press, 2009). See also Joseph R. Washington Jr., *Anti-Blackness in English Religion, 1500–1800* (New York: Edwin Mellon Press, 1984), 309–11. This book chronicles white supremacy in Puritan and Reformed religious thought. For a more directed look at white supremacy in the Calvinist tradition, particularly in the Northern states, see Joseph R. Washington Jr., *Puritan Race Virtue, Vice, and Values, 1620–1820: Original Calvinist True Believers' Enduring Faith and Ethics Race Claims (in Emerging Congregationalist, Presbyterian, and Baptist Power Denominations)* (New York: Peter Lang, 1987).

2. Anthony Bradley, "American Reformed Christianity: a comfortable safe haven for racists?," *The Institute* (blog), July 2, 2010, http://bradley.chattablogs.com/archives/2010/07/american-reform.html.

3. Ken Jubber, "The Prodigal Church: South Africa's Dutch Reformed Church and the Apartheid Policy," *Social Compass* 32, no. 2–3 (1985): 273–85. Peter J. Paris, "The African and African-American Understanding of Our Common Humanity: A Critique of Abraham Kuyper's Anthropology," in *Religion, Pluralism, and Public Life*, ed. Luis E. Lugo (Grand Rapids: Eerdmans, 2000), 263–80. R. L. Dabney, *A Defense of Virginia and the South* (Berryville, VA: Hess Publications, 1998).

4. See the sources cited in note 1. See also Mark A. Noll, *The Civil War as a Theological Crisis* (Chapel Hill, NC: University of North Carolina Press, 2006).

5. Slade, *Open Friendship in a Closed Society*, 107–10.

6. Ibid., 98–100.

7. Ibid., 99.

8. Ibid., 103.

9. Ibid., 107.

10. Ibid., 109.

11. Ibid., 110–12.

12. "Racial Reconciliation," 30th General Assembly, 2002, 30–53, III, Items 14–16, pp. 262–70, http://www.pcahistory.org/pca/race.html.

13. Special thanks to Luke Smith for pointing me to the recent work at Independent Presbyterian Church.

14. Stephen R. Haynes, "Memphis 'kneel-ins' tested churches," *Faith and Leadership*, April 24, 2012, http://www.faithandleadership.com/content /stephen-r-haynes-memphis-kneel-ins-tested-churches?page =full&print=true. This story is catalogued in detail by Haynes in *The Last Segregated Hour: The Memphis Kneel-Ins and the Campaign for Southern Church Desegregation* (New York: Oxford University Press, 2012).

15. Sam Graham, address to the congregation of Independent Presbyterian Church, May 13, 2012, http://mail.indepres.org/media/May 13Sessionwords.pdf.

16. "Regent University Names New President," CBN News, November 3, 2009, http://www.cbn.com/cbnnews/us/2009/November/Regent -University-Announces-New-President.

17. Thanks to Matthew Soerens for the information about Fresno Pacific University.

18. According to the National Council of Churches' *Yearbook of American and Canadian Churches* for 2007: "Yearbook of American and Canadian Churches reports on record number of national church bodies," National Council of Churches, March 5, 2007, http://www .ncccusa.org/news/070305yearbook2007.html.

19. Soong-Chan Rah, *The Next Evangelicalism: Freeing the Church from Western Cultural Captivity* (Downers Grove, IL: IVP Books, 2009).

20. Mike Dorning, "Minority Population Growth Demands Better Education, Groups Say," Bloomberg.com, June 11, 2010. http://www.bloomberg.com/news/2010-06-11/minority-population-growth-demands-better-u-s-education-researchers-say.html.

21. Soong-Chan Rah, "Growing Diversity among America's Children and Youth: Spatial and Temporal Dimensions," *Population and Development Review* 34, no. 2 (2010): 327–46. According to the figures analyzed by the University of New Hampshire in a new demographic study, white women increasingly are delaying having children and are having smaller families, while growing numbers of Hispanic women are having large families at conventional childbearing ages. As these trends continue, America will likely have a white minority by 2050. "Census projections suggest America may become a minority-majority country by the middle of the century," said Kenneth Johnson, a sociology professor at New Hampshire. According to the report, whites currently make up two-thirds of the total US population, but the number of white women of prime childbearing age—20–39 years old—is in decline, dropping 19 percent from 1990.

22. Anthony Bradley, "Freeing the PCA from white, Western (and Southern) Cultural Captivity: A Rahian Analysis," *The Institute* (blog), May 25, 2010, http://bradley.chattablogs.com/archives/2010/05/freeing-the-pca.html#more. I would highly recommend using Rah's book to perform a racial analysis of any denomination or association to evaluate its cultural captivity and place in global Christianity.

23. Rah, *The Next Evangelicalism*, 13. See also Philip Jenkins, *The Next Christendom* (New York: Oxford University Press, 2002).

24. Lausanne Committee for World Evangelization, "The Pasadena Consultation—Homogeneous Unit Principle," *Lausanne Occasional Papers* (The Lausanne Movement, 1978). http://www.lausanne.org/all-documents/lop-1.html.

25. Rowland Croucher et. al., "Church Growth and Pastoral Stress," John Mark Ministries, May 23, 2002, http://jmm.aaa.net.au/articles/9680.htm.

26. Rah, *The Next Evangelicalism*, 16–18.

27. Ibid., 120.

28. Ibid., 121.

29. Quoted in ibid., 72.

30. Ibid.

31. Ibid.

32. Ibid., 144–45.

33. John Piper, *Bloodlines: Race, Cross, and the Christian* (Wheaton, IL: Crossway, 2011). "Race and the Christian," a discussion on race I moderated with Tim Keller and John Piper, was filmed live on March 28, 2012, in New York City and can be accessed at DesiringGod.com.

Chapter Two: Black Pastoral Leadership and Church Planting

1. "Not in Kansas Anymore," *The Wizard of Oz*, directed by Victor Fleming (1939; Burbank, CA: Warner Home Video, 2009), DVD.

Chapter Three: Race and Racialization in Post-Racist Evangelicalism: A View from Asian America

1. A more appropriate title might have been "Race and Racialization: Aspiring Toward a Post-Racist Evangelicalism," thus reflecting the ideal toward which we are straining. However, while I want to emphasize racism, thus including the word *racist*, I am optimistic about the future, thus adding the prefix *post*. For similar aspirations, see Kenneth A. Mathews and M. Sydney Park, *The Post-Racial Church: A Biblical Framework for Multiethnic Reconciliation* (Grand Rapids: Kregel Academic and Professional, 2011).

2. This would be part of the legacy of the processes set in place and extended by the practices of European colonization, the theological aspects of which have been most recently documented by Willie James Jennings, *The Christian Imagination: Theology and the Origins of Race* (New Haven: Yale University Press, 2010).

3. These more racially inflected thoughts should be read alongside two other autobiographical pieces, the first more intellectually oriented, and the other vocationally focused: Amos Yong, "Between the Local and the Global: Autobiographical Reflections on the Emergence of the Global Theological Mind," in *Shaping a Global Theological Mind*, ed. Darren C. Marks (Aldershot, UK: Ashgate, 2008), 187–94, and Amos Yong, "The Spirit, Vocation, and the Life of the Mind: A Pentecostal Testimony," in *The Stories of Pentecostal Scholars*, ed. Steven M. Fettke and Robby C. Waddell (Cleveland, TN: CPT Press, 2012), 203–20.

4. I survey the literature on the diversity of Asian America in "Asian-American Religion: A Review Essay," *Nova Religio: The Journal of Alternative and Emergent Religions* 9, no. 3 (2006): 92–107.

5. I am also playing off Sharon Betcher's "theology on the slant"—presented throughout her book *Spirit and the Politics of Disablement* (Minneapolis: Fortress Press, 2007)—developed in order to show how disability perspectives and a theology of the Holy Spirit can be brought together to reconsider classical theological topics that have worked to marginalize and even oppress people with disabilities. I myself have developed a pneumatological theology of disability in other books—e.g., *The Bible, Disability, and the Church: A New Vision of the People of God* (Grand Rapids: Eerdmans, 2011)—but hope at some point to address this matter with regard to the Asian and Asian-American ecclesial life.

6. The richness of the "reverse mission" from Fuzhou, China, and West Africa are brilliantly documented, respectively, by Kenneth J. Guest, *God in Chinatown: Religion and Survival in New York's Evolving Immigrant Community* (New York: New York University Press, 2003), and Mark Gornik, *Word Made Global: Stories of African Christianity in New York City* (Grand Rapids: Eerdmans, 2011).

7. This understanding was promulgated not only by missionaries in Asia and the Global South, but also in America, among Native Americans; see Kirk Dombrowski, *Against Culture: Development, Politics, and Religion in Indian Alaska* (Lincoln: University of Nebraska Press, 2001).

8. The classic discussion that shows the deep faults and flaws of the "model minority" stereotype is Frank H. Wu, *Yellow: Race in America beyond Black and White* (New York: Basic Books, 2002), 59–77.

9. My *doktorvater*, Robert Cummings Neville, has worked hard as a systematic philosopher and theologian over the decades to engage Eastern traditions, beginning with *Soldier, Sage, Saint* (New York: Fordham University Press, 1978), and *The Tao and the Daimon: Segments of a Religious Inquiry* (Albany: State University of New York Press, 1982).

10. One of these contested questions was whether open theism, advocated by my then colleague Gregory Boyd, fit within the evangelical landscape. I contributed to this discussion a number of essays and articles on the doctrine of divine foreknowledge, the classical version of which open theists reject. This whole debate, which raged not only at

Bethel but also in the Evangelical Theological Society, illuminated for me some of the reasons why, although I count myself as an evangelical on many fronts, there are those who consider themselves guardians of the camp who would question my commitments.

11. My own book on the topic is slowly coming along, with the working title *Evangelical Theology in the Twenty-first Century: Soundings from the Asian-American Diaspora* (Downers Grove, IL: InterVarsity Press, 2014).

12. My Chinese-Mexican-American children live out what Brian Bantum calls "mulattic existence," which simultaneously gives us a window into God's identity in Christ; see Bantum, *Redeeming Mulatto: A Theology of Race and Christian Hybridity* (Waco, TX: Baylor University Press, 2010).

13. I elaborate on these issues in "The Im/Migrant Spirit: De/Constructing a Pentecostal Theology of Migration" in *Theology and Migration in World Christianity: Contextual Perspectives*, vol. 2: *Theology of Migration in the Abrahamic Religions*, ed. Peter C. Phan and Elaine Padilla (Christianities of the World 2; New York: Palgrave Macmillan, 2013), and "Informality, Illegality, and Improvisation: Theological Reflections on Money, Migration, and Ministry in Chinatown, NYC, and Beyond," *Journal of Race, Ethnicity, and Religion* 3, no. 2 (2012) http://www.raceandreligion.com/JRER/Volume_3_%282012%29.html.

14. It will not be easy to digest the retelling of the genealogy of modern evangelical theology in the light of race—e.g., J. Kameron Carter, *Race: A Theological Account* (Oxford: Oxford University Press, 2008)—but it is imperative if repentance and reconciliation are to be possible.

15. Peter C. Phan and Jung Young Lee, eds., *Journeys at the Margin: Toward an Autobiographical Theology in Asian-American Perspective* (Collegeville, MN: Liturgical Press, 1999) is a collection of moving reflections by Asian-American scholars on their own racialization in America and of their struggles to reconcile that with life betwixt and between Asia and America.

16. Fumitaka Matsuoka, "The Church in a Racial-Minority Situation," *Theological Approaches to Christian Education*, ed. Jack L. Seymour and Donald E. Miller (Nashville: Abingdon Press, 1990), 102–21.

17. I sketch a way forward for Pentecostal perspectives on, and contributions to, evangelical theology in two articles: "The Future of Asian Pentecostal Theology: An Asian-American Assessment," *Asian Journal of Pentecostal Studies* 10, no.1 (2007): 22–41; "The Future of Evangelical Theology: Asian and Asian-American Interrogations," *The Asia Journal of Theology* 21, no. 2 (October 2007): 371–97, reprinted by *SANACS Journal* [*Society of Asian North American Christian Studies Journal*] 1 (2009): 5–27.

18. Already noted by Lester-Edwin J. Ruiz and Eleazar S. Fernandez, "What Do We Do with the Diversity That We Already Are?: The Asian and Asian North American in Accredited Graduate Theological Education," *Theological Education* 45, no. 1 (2009): 41–58. I provide an overview of the difficult problem of categorizing Asian-American evangelical theology in "Whither Asian-American Evangelical Theology? What Asian? Which American? Whose *Evangelion*?" *Evangelical Review of Theology* 32, no. 1 (2008): 22–37.

19. The theological challenges faced by Asian-American evangelicals are detailed in my essays, "Asian-American Historicity: The Problem and Promise of Evangelical Theology," *SANACS Journal* 4 (2012), and "Asian-American Evangelical Theology," in *Global Theology in Evangelical Perspective: Exploring the Contextual Nature of Theology and Mission*, ed. Jeffrey Greenman and Gene L. Green (Downers Grove, IL: Inter-Varsity Press, 2012), 195–209.

20. E.g., Limatula Longkumer, "Women in Theological Education from an Asian Perspective," *Handbook of Theological Education in World Christianity: Theological Perspectives, Ecumenical Trends, Regional Surveys*, ed. Dietrich Werner, David Esterline, Namsoon Kang, and Joshva Raja (Eugene, OR: Wipf & Stock, 2010), 68–75.

21. Many Asian-Americans are already engaged in this important and vital task—e.g., D. J. Chuang and Timothy Tseng, eds., *Conversations: Asian-American Evangelical Theologies in Formation* (Washington: L2 Foundation, 2006); Viji Nakka-Cammauf and Timothy Tseng, eds., *Asian-American Christianity: A Reader* (Castro Valley, CA: Pacific Asian-American and Canadian Christian Education Project, and the Institute for the Study of Asian-American Christianity, 2009); Young Lee Hertig and Chloe Sun, eds., *Mirrored Reflections: Reframing Biblical*

Characters (Eugene, OR: Wipf & Stock, 2010); and Jonathan Y. Tan, *Introducing Asian-American Theologies* (Maryknoll, NY: Orbis Books, 2008), esp. ch. 9.

22. Thanks to the following for the helpful comments on a previous draft of this paper: Grace Kim (Moravian Theological Seminary), Antipas Harris (Regent University), and Bernon Lee (Bethel University, St. Paul, Minnesota). I thank also my graduate assistant, Vincent Le, for proofreading my paper. And I am grateful for Anthony Bradley's invitation to contribute to this important volume. None of them, however, should be held responsible for the opinions expressed here.

Chapter Four: Serving Alongside Latinos in a Multiethnic, Transnational, Rapidly Changing World

1. Both *Hispanic* and *Latino* are used to group people who have a common background in the Spanish-speaking world. Both terms are problematic for various reasons, though some insist on using one or the other. Others use a composite like *Hispanic/Latino* to try to include all people. At Fuller Seminary, we decided to use both, one in English and the other in Spanish. So I direct the "Hispanic Center" in English, but the "Centro Latino" in Spanish. We chose to do it this way because of gender issues in the way the term *Latino* is used in English, though it is a Spanish word. *Hispanic* does not have that problem, since it is an English word.

2. The 1970 census introduced the term *Hispanic* to describe all people from the Spanish-speaking world. Before that, all of us in the Southwest were *Mexicans*. It did not matter where we were born. After the US takeover of the Southwest in 1848, "we" all became foreigners, "Mexicans." This usage remained common well into the 1980s and beyond. For example, when Olga and I started pastoring in Parlier, California, the church we pastored was considered a "Mexican" church, even though half the congregation was US-born and a few, like my wife, did not have a Mexican background.

3. My parents, my wife, and I attended Río Grande Bible Institute in Edinburg, Texas. To this date Latino pastors are more likely to have been trained at Latino Bible Institutes than at a seminary.

4. I also remember being in denominational meetings where racially charged jokes, usually aimed at African-Americans, were considered acceptable lunchtime fare.

5. John Denver, "Rocky Mountain High" recorded August 1972 on *Rocky Mountain High*.

6. See Samuel Huntington, *Who Are We?: The Challenges to America's National Identity* (New York: Simon & Schuster, 2005).

7. In *Walk with the People: Latino Ministry in the United States* (Nashville: Abingdon, 2008), I describe some of those complexities and their impact on ministry among Latinos.

8. Jeffrey Passel and D'Vera Cohn, "U.S. Population Projections: 2005–2050," Pew Research Hispanic Center, February 11, 2008, http://pew hispanic.org/reports/report.php?ReportID=85.

9. That is the basic premise of Juan González, *Harvest of Empire: A History of Latinos in America* (New York: Viking, 2000). According to González, Latinos are a part of the United States primarily because of US intervention and expansion into Latin America.

10. The Presbyterian College of the Southwest was started 1884 in Del Norte, Colorado, largely through the efforts of missionaries in the area. In 1890, it began a pastoral education program for Spanish-speaking people. It graduated several generations of leaders who influenced Presbyterian ministry throughout the first half of the twentieth century. The school closed in 1901 due to a lack of funds. (See my book *Sea la Luz: The Making of Mexican Protestantism in the American Southwest, 1829–1900* [Denton: University of North Texas Press, 2006], 112–14.)

11. The common complaint was that students were formed to effectively pastor a "white, suburban" church, and that they were socialized into expecting the type of salary that that type of church can provide. From the perspective of Latino churches, they were effectively educated out of the community. Many pastors returned to the community, but no longer seemed to fit. Others accepted calls in "white, suburban" churches.

12. See the study "Changing Faiths: Latinos and the Transformation of American Religion," Pew Research Hispanic Center, April 25, 2007, http://pewhispanic.org/reports/report.php?ReportID=75.

13. ATS is the seminary accrediting association for the United States, Canada, and Puerto Rico.

14. See Justo González, *Santa Biblia: The Bible Through Hispanic Eyes* (Nashville: Abingdon Press, 1996).

15. This document was written in 1983, under the leadership of then president David Hubbard, to comment upon Fuller's mission statement and to demonstrate how Fuller's specific mission of training leaders fits into the larger mission of what God is doing in the world. It is available at http://www.fuller.edu/page.aspx?id=434 &terms=mission+beyond+the+mission.

16. Jehu Hanciles has written an excellent book on the impact of migration on the church in the West. See *Beyond Christendom: Globalization, African Migration and the Transformation of the West* (Maryknoll, NY: Orbis Books, 2008).

17. Mark Lau Branson and Juan F. Martínez, *Churches, Cultures and Leadership: A Practical Theology of Congregations and Ethnicities* (Downers Grove, IL: IVP Academic, 2011).

18. See "From Hospitality to Shalom" in Elizabeth Conde-Frazier, S. Steve Kang, and Gary A. Parrett, *A Many Colored Kingdom: Multicultural Dynamics for Spiritual Formation* (Grand Rapids: Baker Academic, 2004), 167–210.

19. Because very few Latino students study at US seminaries, they are often expected to "represent" the whole of the community, though they can only effectively represent their own experiences.

Chapter Five: Ethnic Scarcity in Evangelical Theology: Where Are the Authors?

1. Vincent Bacote, "When Will There Be Room in the Inn? Minorities and Evangelical Leadership Development," *Urban Mission*, December 1994, 25–33.

2. This was not the only complaint, but definitely the most illuminating one for me at the time.

3. Of course, evangelical theology is not gnostic in the sense of regarding materiality as evil or denying the Incarnation, but some might sense gnostic tendencies in the failure to acknowledge the particularity of African-Americans under the guise of simply seeing

everyone as the same, regardless of race or ethnicity, when in fact this is a failure to actually see persons in their fullness.

4. "ETS Constitution," The Evangelical Theological Society, December 28, 1949, http://www.etsjets.org/about/constitution.

5. For example, John Perkins participated in a panel at the New Orleans annual meeting, and this author presented a paper in another section at the same meeting.

6. Ed Gilbreath, *Reconciliation Blues: A Black Evangelical's Inside View of White Christianity* (Downers Grove, IL: InterVarsity Press, 2006). Also see Michael O. Emerson and Christian Smith, *Divided by Faith: Evangelical Religion and the Problem of Race in America* (New York: Oxford University Press, 2000).

7. Financial support is important, but here I refer to much more: the spiritual, social, and emotional support such students often need, even in a purportedly "post-racial" era.

Chapter Six: Blacks and Latinos in Theological Education as Professors and Administrators

1. Recent attempts to broaden the scope of American evangelicalism— nicely detailed, e.g., in Peter Goodwin Heltzel's important text, *Jesus and Justice: Evangelicals, Race, and American Politics* (New Haven: Yale University Press, 2009)—are well meaning but have little institutional relevance. The educational institutions that consider themselves part of American evangelicalism do not evince the adoption of such a broadening of perspective, based on their requirements for doctrinal assent as a condition of participation.

2. See Thabiti M. Anyabwile, *The Decline of African American Theology* (Downers Grove, IL: IVP Academic, 2007). Anyabwile's introduction to African-American Christian thought loses its value because he insists on using Reformed theology, in form and doctrine, as the barometer of truth.

3. Rather than cite all the literature here, I refer the reader to two studies cited in my essay. The first, Beverly Absher's "Attraction and Retention of Females and Minorities in Christian Higher Education," in *Journal of Research on Christian Education* 18 (2009): 160–89, focuses on faculty in Christian colleges and universities and has a helpful

bibliography. The second, "Faculty of Color in Academe: What 20 Years of Literature Tells Us," by Caroline Sotello Viernes Turner, Juan Carlos Gonzalez, and J. Luke Wood, in *Journal of Diversity in Higher Education* 1, no. 3 (2008): 139–68 reviews research on faculty at a number of institutions. Their findings confirm the commonality of challenges in both evangelical and nonsectarian colleges and universities with respect to black and Latino faculty. They provide a lengthy bibliography in which we can see the parallels between the challenges. I would add two essays I wrote while working with faculty at evangelical colleges in the 1990s: "Multiculturalism and Christian Liberal Arts," *Gordon College Occasional Papers* (1991), and "New Covenant and Good News: What's a Nice Hue like You Doing in a Place like This?" in *Multicultural Congress on Access and Equity: A Conference for People in Christian Higher Education*, The Christian College Coalition (1994).

4. I used this title for an essay I wrote for what was then *ESA Magazine*, now *Prism: America's Alternative Evangelical Voice* 3, no. 7 (1996). Adapted from a paper I presented at the first William Bentley Institute for Black Evangelical Theology in 1993, I put forth there the tension between doctrinal understandings of Christian faith as espoused by evangelicalism and relational understandings of Christianity in the black church tradition.

5. Theodore Cross and Robert Bruce Slater, "Black Enrollment at the Nation's Colleges and Universities Are on the Rise," in *Christian Higher Education* 3 (2004): 391–99. This article was reprinted with permission from the *Journal of Blacks in Higher Education* 43 (Spring 2004): 21–24.

6. Cross and Slater, "Black Enrollment."

7. Absher, "Attraction and Retention of Females and Minorities."

8. See Donald Dayton, *Discovering an Evangelical Heritage* (Peabody, MA: Hendrickson Press, 1988), which traces this development with nuance and thoroughness. Later efforts to look at this connection include Mark A. Noll, *God and Race in American Politics: A Short History* (Princeton, NJ: Princeton University Press, 2010), and Michael O. Emerson and Christian Smith, *Divided by Faith: Evangelical Religion and the Problem of Race in America* (Oxford: Oxford University Press, 2000).

9. See his account in the opening chapter of *Soul Theology: The Heart of Black Culture*, coauthored with Henry Mitchell (Nashville: Abingdon, 1991).

10. S. J. Roels, "The Business Ethics of Evangelicals," *Business Ethics Quarterly* 7, no. 2 (March 1997): 109–22.

11. Trulear, "Somewhere to Lay My Head," *ESA Magazine* 3, no. 7 (1996).

12. Absher, "Attraction and Retention of Females and Minorities."

Chapter Seven: Blacks and Latinos in Theological Education as Students

1. "Black Student College Graduation Rates Inch Higher But a Large Racial Gap Persists," *Journal of Blacks in Higher Education*, accessed March 17, 2011, http://www.jbhe.com/preview/winter 07preview.html.

2. "Fact Book," Nyack College, Fall 2011, http://nyack.edu/files /NYACK_FACTBOOK_2011.pdf.

3. Franklyn Jenifer, "Minorities and Women in Higher Education and the Role of Mentoring in Their Advancement," 4, accessed March 17, 2011, http://www.utsystem.edu/aca/files/Mentorship.pdf.

4. Ibid.

5. "Why Minority Students Do Not Graduate from College," *Newsweek*, accessed March 17, 2011, www.newsweek.com/2010/02/18 /minority-report.html.

6. Ibid.

7. Terese Kreuzer, "Computers on Campus: The Black-White Technology Gap," *The Journal of Blacks in Higher Education*, 1 (Fall 1993), 88–95.

8. Faculty Career Exploration program brochure retrieved from http://www.rit.edu/academicaffairs/facultyrecruitment/docs/FFCEP brochure.pdf.

9. "Program Promotes Higher Minority Graduation Rates," PBS, September 29, 2010, http://www.pbs.org/newshour/extra/video /blog/2010/09/program_promotes_higher_minori.html.

10. Jenifer, "Minorities and Women in Higher Education."

Chapter Eight: A Black Church Perspective on Minorities in Evangelicalism

1. Lutheran Church—Missouri Synod, "Racism and the Church" (1994), 1.

2. Ibid., 42.

3. Patricia Hill Collins, *Fighting Words: Black Women and the Search for Justice* (Minneapolis: University of Minnesota Press, 1998), 5.

4. Kenneth Scott LaTourette, *A History of Christianity, Volume I: to A.D. 1500* (New York: Harper & Row, 1975), 19.

5. Thomas Oden, *How Africa Shaped the Christian Mind: Rediscovering the African Seedbed of Western Christianity* (Downers Grove, IL: InterVarsity Press, 2007), 97.

6. LaTourette, *A History of Christianity*, 77.

7. Oden, *How Africa Shaped the Christian Mind*, 28.

8. Ibid., 49.

9. Tibebe Eshete, *The Evangelical Movement in Ethiopia: Resistance and Resilience* (Waco, TX: Baylor University Press, 2009), 15.

10. Archbishop Yeseha, *The Ethiopian Tewahedo Church: An Integrally African Church* (Nashville: J. C. Winston Pub. Co., 1997), xiii.

11. Robert E. Hood, *Must God Remain Greek?: Afro Cultures and God-Talk* (Minneapolis: Augsburg Fortress, 1990), 1–10.

12. Oden, *How Africa Shaped the Christian Mind*, 28.

13. Philip Jenkins, *The Next Christendom: The Coming of Global Christianity* (New York: Oxford University Press, 2007), 1.

14. Soong-Chan Rah, *The Next Evangelicalism: Freeing the Church from Western Cultural Captivity* (Downers Grove, IL: InterVarsity Press, 2009), 13.

Chapter Nine: Theology and Cultural Awareness Applied: Discipling Urban Men

1. Tupac Shakur attempts to describe a "thug" in a positive way:

> When I say thug I mean not a criminal, someone who beats you over the head, I mean the underdog. . . . If [a] person who has nothing succeeds, he's a thug. Cuz he overcame all the obstacles. . . . It doesn't have anything to do with the dictionary's version of thug. . . .

To me thug is my pride. . . . Not being someone who goes against the law. Not being someone that takes, but being someone that has nothing and even though there is no home for me to go to, my head is up high, my chest is out, I walk tall, I talk loud. . . . I'm being strong. I don't understand why America doesn't understand thug life. America is thug life. What makes me saying "I don't give a f—" different than Patrick Henry saying, "Give me liberty or give me death"? (Tupac Shakur, Afeni Shakur, and Walter Einenkel, *Tupac Shakur* [New York: Simon and Schuster, 2003], 122)

2. A hoopdie is a substandard car that has two or more of these characteristics, according to UrbanDictionary.com: (1) It has been crashed and never been to a body shop. (2) It has rust everywhere. (3) It has been painted with a paintbrush. (4) It has home-drawn flames on the side. (5) It has a wooden spoiler made in the backyard and nailed to the trunk. (6) It has racing numbers, even though it couldn't possibly race. (7) It has a fake engine blower nailed to the hood.

3. Leslie Bricusse and Anthony Newley, "The Candy Man" (1971).

4. An illustration used by Henry Mitchell.

Afterword

1. See J. Deotis Roberts, *Liberation and Reconciliation: A Black Theology*, 2nd ed. (Louisville: Westminster John Knox Press, 2005), and John M. Perkins, *Let Justice Roll Down* (New York: Regal, 2006).

2. Peggy McIntosh, "White Privilege: Unpacking the Invisible Knapsack," *Peace and Freedom Magazine*, July–August 1989, 10–12.

3. Joseph Barndt, *Understanding and Dismantling Racism: The Twenty-first Century Challenge to White America* (Minneapolis: Fortress Press, 2007), 96.

4. Gordon W. Allport, *The Nature of Prejudice* (Cambridge, MA: Perseus Books, 1954).

5. "Tim Keller on Churches and Race," Big Think, accessed June 19, 2012, http://bigthink.com/ideas/13308.

6. Richie Sessions, "The Gospel and Race," Independent Presbyterian Church, May 13, 2012, http://media.indepres.org/sermoncatalog /display.asp.

Appendix: Racism and the Church: Overcoming the Idolatry

1. 1992 Resolution 3-03 "To Combat All Racism," 1992 *Proceedings*, 113-14.

2. LC I, 3, 10.

3. LC I, 329.

4. LC II, 2.

5. In their recent study of religion in contemporary American society, summarized in the book *One Nation under God* (New York: Harmony Books, 1993), Barry A. Kosmin and Seymour P. Lachman observe that "numbering nearly 30 million, the African-American population is the nation's largest and, historically, its most important minority. Today it comprises almost 12% of the total U.S. population, a decrease from 20% in 1800." "The most significant ethnic factor in American religion," they point out, is "the historical tradition of a separatist and racially aware black church" (130).

6. Our biblically shaped response to racism must be carefully distinguished from the critique of racism that Christians hold in common with many non-Christian people of good will and which is reflected in this section of the document.

7. *Encyclopedia Britannica*, 15th ed., s.v. "Racism," by Pierre L. van den Berghe.

8. Pierre L. van den Berghe, *Race and Racism* (New York: John Wiley & Sons, Inc., 1967), 11. In his article on "Racism" in *Britannica*, van den Berghe notes that some sociologists distinguish between "racism" and "racialism," applying the former term to the *theory* or *doctrine* of racism and the latter to the actual *practice* of discrimination and prejudice.

9. van den Berghe, *Britannica*.

10. See Joseph Barndt, *Dismantling Racism* (Minneapolis: Augsburg Fortress, 1991), 28-31.

11. When anthropologists today use the term "race," they are most typically referring to some heuristic group under study and are not referring to a "race" as that term is popularly understood. The concept of "race" was initially popularized in western thought by anthropologists. The work done by physical anthropologists later involved in the study of genetics led to the rejection of any serious scientific use of this concept. See Alaka Wali, "Multiculturalism: An Anthropological

Perspective," in *Report from the Institute for Philosophy & Public Policy,* Spring/Summer 1992, 6-8.

12. *The Harper Dictionary of Modern Thought,* 1988 rev. ed., s.v. "Race/Racism," by Michael D. Biddiss.

13. *Encyclopedia of Sociology,* 1993 ed., s.v. "Race," by Susan R. Pitchford.

14. Although trait variation in plants and animals is not regarded as evidence of species differentiation, racists regard this phenomenon in human beings as absolute evidence of species differentiation. Consistent with this view, racists have sought to maintain the racial purity of their particular group and to accomplish this goal through a policy of strict segregation.

15. *The American Heritage Dictionary of the English Language,* 1992 ed., s.v. "Culture."

16. *The Harper Dictionary of Modern Thought* (s.v. "Culture," by Ronald Fletcher) defines "culture" as follows: "the total body of material artifacts (tools, weapons, houses, places of work, worship, government, recreation, works of art, etc.), of collective mental and spiritual 'artifacts' (systems of symbols, ideas, beliefs, aesthetic perceptions, values, etc.), and of distinctive forms of behaviour (institutions, groupings, rituals, modes of organization, etc.) created by a people (sometimes deliberately, sometimes through unforeseen interconnections and consequences) in their ongoing activities within their particular life-conditions, and (though undergoing kinds and degrees of change) transmitted from generation to generation" (195).

17. *Encyclopedia of Anthropology,* 1976, s.v., "Acculturation," 1-2. This is not to say, of course, that the behavior patterns and cultural traditions upon which a person depends for survival are in every case morally acceptable. Viewed according to the standard of God's will for human beings, some cultural practices are evil.

18. van den Berghe, *Britannica.*

19. Carey McWilliams, *Brothers under the Skin* (Boston: Little, Brown and Company, 1964), 140-69.

20. This new identity ultimately consisted of restricting the definition of "humanity" to whites and was codified in the law of the land. For example, Chief Justice Roger Brooke Taney of the U.S. Supreme Court ended his famous Dred Scott decision of 1857 by saying that "he

had no ground to assert that Negroes were not 'beings of an inferior order . . . so far inferior that they had no rights which the white man was bound to respect.'" Pierre L. van den Berghe, *Race and Racism*, 78.

21. See van den Berghe, *Race and Racism*, and other basic texts on racial and ethnic minorities for discussions of this distinction.

22. William Graham Sumner, *Folkways* (Boston: Ginn and Company, 1906), 13.

23. In emic analysis, "the subjects one is studying have their own (folk) categories (cognitive categories), assumptions about those categories, taxonomies and part-whole systems in terms of which they logically relate these categories to each other, as well as values concerning items classified according to these categories. To understand the behavior of subjects, then, it is crucial that the field researcher identify the cognitive properties of these emic categories; otherwise interpretation of behavior cannot claim to reflect units of behavior which are meaningful to the people studied" (*Encyclopedia of Anthropology*, s.v. "Emics," 142). "Emic analyses are therefore those which stress the subjective meanings shared by a social group and their culturally specific model of experience" (*Dictionary of Anthropology*, 1986, s.v. "emic/etic," 92).

24. While the terms "majority" and "minority" have widely accepted and legitimate usage in professional literature, in popular discourse they often provide an example of the language of prejudice. Those who use these terms today are rarely conscious of the fact that they and other terms like them are indeed a part of the language of prejudice.

The particular set of relationships that majority/minority groups have is frequently related to the number of minority groups in a given society. If there is only one minority group in a given society, it is likely to absorb all of the anxieties and frustrations of the dominant group and become the object of many of its power manipulations. If there are several minority groups (as in American society), they will be ranked, and quite often the majority will play one minority group off against another. This was done most conspicuously in the Hawaiian Islands. Not infrequently, this will affect the way in which minorities respond to each other.

The pioneering work in the ranking of minority groups has been conducted by Emory S. Bogardus in his development of the Social

Distance Scale. Prejudice, as Bogardus sees it, is a special case of social distance. See Emory S. Bogardus, *A Forty Year Racial Distance Study* (Los Angeles: University of Southern California, 1967).

25. Still regarded as a standard reference is Gordon Allport, *The Nature of Prejudice* (Garden City, NY: Doubleday & Company, Inc., 1954). See pages 1-79 for a basic discussion of the nature of prejudice.

26. While a stereotype frequently accompanies prejudice, it should not be confused with prejudice. "Whether favorable or unfavorable, *a stereotype is an exaggerated belief associated with a category. Its function is to justify (rationalize) our conduct in relation to that category,*" and it is usually sustained by selective forgetting (Allport, *The Nature of Prejudice*, 187). Not all stereotypes, of course, are false, nor do they necessarily have a negative function or purpose. Blacks may well jump higher than Asians and Norwegians are probably taller than Mexicans, but such generalizations are harmless as long as they involve no judgment as to the relative worth or merit of groups being so compared. Over time stereotypes may change, but the underlying prejudice does not. Thus, attacking stereotypes alone will not eradicate the roots of prejudice.

27. "One of the biggest misconceptions about intergroup relations is that prejudice and discrimination can only occur jointly (Simpson & Yinger, 1965). But, as Merton (1976) noted, there are four, not two, possible relationships between prejudice and discrimination: (1) the presence of both, (2) the absence of both of them, (3) prejudice without discrimination, and (4) discrimination without prejudice.

"Virtually all the attention of commentators on intergroup relations has been on the first two relationships. This undue concentration on the joint presence or absence of prejudice and discrimination makes the latter two relationships—prejudice without discrimination and discrimination without prejudice—appear as anomalies. Prejudice without discrimination refers to situations in which prejudiced persons do not 'act out' their intolerant attitudes because of such external constraints as the threat of formal sanctions (for example, civil right laws, affirmative action mandates, or judicial injunctions) or the fear of informal sanctions (for example, social ostracism) by unprejudiced colleagues, neighbors, or friends.

"Similarly, discrimination without prejudice occurs when unprejudiced persons manifest discriminatory behavior out of fear of informal sanctions (such as ostracism, harassment, physical assault, property destruction) from prejudiced colleagues, neighbors, and friends; laws, policies, and other formal practices that legitimize or condone intolerant behavior; or ignorance, when individuals are unaware that their actions have discriminatory effects or consequences" (*Encyclopedia of Social Work*, 18th edition, s.v. "Racism," 1:946).

28. Cf. Judith Lichtenberg, "Racism in the Head, Racism in the World," in *Report from the Institute for Philosophy & Public Policy*, Spring/Summer 1992, 3-5.

29. Alan Davies, "The Ideology of Racism," in *The Church and Racism*, Gregory Baum and John Coleman, eds. (New York: The Seabury Press, 1982), 11. Concerning racism as an *ideology*, the *Dictionary of the Ecumenical Movement* (1991, s.v. "Racism") states the following: "In recent years an effort has been made to distinguish between racialism and racism. One can understand racialism to be the use of racial or ethnocentric characteristics to determine value or access or participation and, by the same token, to exclude others from such. Racialism may not necessarily be value-laden as such. It does not say that one person is better than another because of race but simply that one chooses not to associate with people on account of their race. But racism has become a political ideology, on the basis of which the social reality is being interpreted and political and economic decisions made. In essence a racist ideology attaches value to ethnocentric characteristics and seeks to maintain deterministic relations between biological characteristics and cultural attributes. However, one must not lose sight of the fact that, ultimately, racism is about power. As an ideology it is the means whereby the dominant group, as determined by racial characteristics, imposes its will upon others so as to exclude them from effective participation in decision making and to exploit them for economic gain."

In this connection, see also Shelby Steele, *The Content of Our Character* (St. Martin's Press, 1990; repr. New York: HarperCollins Publishers, 1991), in which Steele argues that race should not be a source of power or advantage or disadvantage for anyone in a free society. He rejects the "marriage" of race and power.

30. Davies, "The Ideology of Racism," 15. See also Lichtenberg, "Racism in the Head, Racism in the World."

31. See James M. Jones, "The Concept of Racism and Its Changing Reality," in Benjamin P. Bowser and Raymand G. Hung's *Impacts of Racism on White Americans* (Beverly Hills, CA: Sage Publications, 1981), 27ff. See also Barndt, *Dismantling Racism*, for distinctions between "individual," "institutional," and "cultural" racism (51-122).

32. van den Berghe, *Britannica*.

33. Ibid.

34. See Alan Davies, "The Ideology of Racism," 11-15; also Alan Davies, *Infected Christianity: A Study of Modern Racism* (Kingston and Montreal: McGill-Queen's University Press, 1988), 3-26; van den Berghe, *Race and Racism*, 17-21; 77-95.

35. van den Berghe, *Race and Racism*, 77-78.

36. Israel Acrelius, *A History of New Sweden* (Philadelphia: The Historical Society of Pennsylvania, 1874), viii.

37. Julius F. Sachse, *Justus Falckner: Mystic and Scholar* (Philadelphia, 1903), 104.

38. Harry J. Kreider, *Lutheranism in Colonial New York* (New York: Edwards Brothers, Inc., 1942), 56.

39. Ibid.

40. William Edward Eisenberg, *The Lutheran Church in Virginia 1717-1962* (Roanoke, Virginia: The Trustees of the Virginia Synod, Lutheran Church in America, 1967), 13.

41. Ibid., 13–14.

42. While the colony of Georgia was chartered by the English crown, it was initially organized and administered by a group of private citizens known as the Trustees. Their goal was to create a colony where the virtues of the English yeomen could be practiced. One of the laws (established by the Trustees) governing life in the colony was a prohibition on slavery. The Salzburgers' opposition to slavery made them especially welcome in the colony.

43. The colony of Georgia had hardly been formally established (1734) before a number of its citizens began petitioning the Trustees concerning the introduction of slavery. Among other things, they were encouraged to do so because slavery was permitted in all of the

surrounding colonies. The debate about slavery in Georgia became so heated that one observer states that "the whole province dwelt, as it were on the brink of a [revolutionary] volcano" (W. D. Weatherford, *American Churches and The Negro* [Boston: The Christopher Publishing House, 1957], 141). Boltzius, however, continued to oppose the introduction of slavery until 1750.

44. The justification for Boltzius withdrawing his objection to slavery came from his mentor in Germany, the Rev. Samuel Urlsperger. Urlsperger counseled, "If you take slaves in faith, and with the intent of conducting them to Christ, the action will not be a sin, but may prove a benediction" (George Fenwick Jones, *The Georgia Dutch from the Rhine and Danube to the Savannah*, 1733-1783 [Athens and London: The University of Georgia Press, 1992], 268-69).

45. In 1758 Rev. Boltzius' slave Mary gave birth to a female named Christine (Baptism #460, *Jerusalem Recordbook*). Two of the pastors to the Salzburgers, the Revs. Rabenhorst and Lemcke, owned 12 of the 59 young slaves baptized between 1753 and 1781. (See *Jerusalem Recordbook*.)

46. *A History of the Lutheran Church in South Carolina*, prepared and edited by "The History of Synod Committee" (Columbia, SC; The South Carolina Synod of the LCA, 1971), 242.

47. In 1837 the Franckean Synod (a small group of clergy in upper New York) declared itself against pulpit and altar fellowship with any church that had slaveholders. It was joined by the East Ohio and Allegheny Synods in 1844, the Pittsburgh Synod in 1845, the Wittenberg Synod in 1852, and the Synod of Northern Indiana in 1859 (Thomas R. Noon, "Early Black Lutherans in the South [to 1865]," *Concordia Historical Institute Quarterly* 50 [Summer 1977], 52).

48. The person ordained was William Alexander Payne. Payne never served a Lutheran congregation. He subsequently went on to become one of the leading bishops in the African Methodist Episcopal Church. Prior to Payne's ordination, Jehu (John) Jones had been commissioned by the New York Ministerium in 1832 to serve as a Lutheran missionary in Africa. Jones never made it to Africa. He did organize the first all-black Lutheran congregation in 1834, located in Philadelphia, Pennsylvania.

49. Jacob L. Morgan, Bachman S. Brown and John Hall, eds., *History of the Lutheran Church in North Carolina*, published by the authority

of the United Evangelical Lutheran Synod of North Carolina, 1803-1953, n.d., 82.

50. Quoted from Richard C. Dickinson, *Roses and Thorns* (St. Louis: Concordia Publishing House, 1977), 24-25.

51. *Luther's Small Catechism with Explanation*, 1986 edition, 23.

52. At its 1992 convention the Synod adopted Resolution 3-03 " To Combat All Racism," in which it urged its members "to repent of any attitude or practice of racism as individuals and congregations" and resolved that "the Synod repudiate all racism and urge its members to celebrate God's love in Christ and their forgiveness and acceptance as God's children by loving and serving all fellow humans as they have been loved and served, without any exception of persons, and to work toward social justice in their neighborhoods and work places and all areas of society" (1992 *Convention Proceedings*, 114).

53. Alan Davies ("The Ideology of Racism") writes concerning the changing reality of racism, "all pre-war myths of white supremacy (e.g., Afrikanerdom), where they still exist today, seem more as defence mechanisms against the winds of change than as triumphalistic visions of a soon-to-be-realized future. But their demise does *not* mean that racism itself is dead. On the contrary, the rebirth of racism is one of the most ominous signs or our era. Racism, like a Hindu god, may have many incarnations. Precisely because the ideology is no longer respectable, racist views today possess an incognito character, incarnating themselves in systems of social, political and economic power, concealing themselves behind bland bureaucratic facades. This is not so much ideological as 'structural' racism: a racism that need not identify itself as racist, but which can exercise great demonic energy in the world. It is mostly this form of racism that confronts us today. To struggle against it is far harder than to struggle against the unenlightened minds of old-fashioned racists . . ." (15).

54. This is not to suggest that we should avoid dealing with the consequences of racism but look only to the removal of its causes. In some ways, people may feel that they can only deal with the consequences. To use a familiar illustration, if the neighborhood bully is beating up one's child every day and taking his lunch money, the reaction is first to remedy the consequences. Certainly, to sit around

and wait for a change of heart only perpetuates the hurt, while the offender goes unchallenged.

55. Some authorities refer to this as the "victim blame argument." See James M. Jones, "The Concept of Racism and its Changing Reality," 46.

56. For a complete history of developments in this regard, see Jeff G. Johnson, *Black Christians: The Untold Lutheran Story* (St. Louis: Concordia Publishing House, 1991), 198-221; 225-30.

57. The Evangelical Lutheran Synodical Conference of North America (hereafter referred to simply as the Synodical Conference) was an association of independent Lutheran churches organized in 1872 that existed for nearly one hundred years. It originally consisted of the Illinois, Minnesota, Missouri, Norwegian, Ohio, and Wisconsin synods.

The Synodical Conference's entry into Negro mission work appears to have been driven by a crisis and actually was somewhat accidental. Up to the mid-1870s, the Synodical Conference had been involved in foreign mission work in connection with the Leipzig and Hermannsburg Mission Societies in Germany. That arrangement was suddenly terminated because of theological differences between the Synodical Conference and the German mission societies. The Synodical Conference suddenly found itself abruptly cut off from any foreign mission work at a time when its constituency was extremely interested in such endeavors. As the mission committee of the Synodical Conference put it, "If we make no use of the desire of our Lutheran Christians to do something for heathen missions, they will surely apply their money where we would not like to see it go" (F. Dean Lueking, *Mission in the Making* [St. Louis: Concordia Publishing House, 1964], 85).

A mission-minded delegate to the July 1877 convention proposed that the Synodical Conference begin mission work among American Negroes. The resolution was adopted with almost no debate. Within three months of the passage of that resolution, a missionary had been commissioned and sent out to survey the field.

The Synodical Conference appeared to be unaware of the fact that there was a black constituency in the United States. Before the Civil War, there had been thousands of black Lutherans in the South. At the very moment when the Synodical Conference was trying to decide where to begin its work among black people, the Lutheran synods of the South were trying to get some Lutheran body to take over the work that they had been conducting for over half a century. The Synodical Conference finally made contact with those black Lutherans when, in 1891, the Evangelical Lutheran Alpha Synod of Freedmen in America invited the Synodical Conference into North Carolina.

58. The Synodical Conference began training African Americans for the teaching and pastoral ministry as early as 1882 at Addison, Illinois, and at Concordia Seminary in Springfield, Illinois. Shortly after Immanuel Lutheran College and Seminary in Greensboro, North Carolina, opened in 1903, the Synodical Conference passed a rule requiring all black persons who were preparing for professional church work to be trained at Immanuel. This regulation apparently had nothing to do with the ability of African American students to function at Addison or Concordia Seminary, Springfield, inasmuch as a number of blacks had functioned quite successfully at those institutions for over twenty years. Required attendance at Immanuel also had little to do with the ministry in the black community because no white pastor or teacher working in the black community was required to attend Immanuel, not even for orientation. The regulation was based solely on the color of one's skin.

Luther College in New Orleans was closed in 1925 after having graduated only one student in its twenty-two year history. Immanuel was closed in 1961. Selma Academy (now Concordia College Selma) still exists and at the date of this writing is in the process of becoming a four-year educational institution.

Minority group students began enrolling in Missouri Synod schools before the 1947 decision to grant black pastors and congregations membership in the Synod. Concordia Seminary, St. Louis, admitted an African American student in 1944 and graduated a Japanese American student in 1945.

59. Some feel that this 1947 action of the Missouri Synod should more properly be called an instance of desegregation, inasmuch as it involved primarily the removal of restrictions on the membership of African Americans within the Synod. We have referred to this action as "integration" because the language of the document leading to the

inclusion of African Americans in the Missouri Synod specifically refers to "integration," not "desegregation."

60. The Synod adopted Resolution 26 "Race Relations in National and World-Wide Church Work," which incorporates Memorial 409 "Establishment of Congregations on a Nonsegregated Basis" (1956 *Proceedings*, 757-59; cf. 753-54).

61. In 1961 the Southern District was the last judicatory within the Missouri Synod to implement the 1947 decision to grant African Americans membership in the Synod.

62. 1977 Resolution 10-01A "To Establish Administration for Black Ministry," 1977 *Proceedings*, 199.

63. These policies, together with the organization of the Synodical Conference Mission Board, ultimately led to the administrative ineffectiveness of that Board. Beginning in 1927 (the 50th anniversary of the Synodical Conference's work among blacks) black pastors and their congregations began petitioning the Synodical Conference for a more effective organizational system for managing black ministry. These petitions continued until 1938 when those involved in black ministry petitioned for the formation of a separate synod. During that same period, approximately 50 percent of the black pastors left the ministry. The largest (geographically and numerically) and most rapidly growing of the three black mission fields (the Eastern Field) of the Synodical Conference extended from the Atlantic to the Pacific coast. Between 1924 and the 1947 decision to integrate black pastors and congregations into the Missouri Synod, the superintendent of the Eastern Field (located in Greensboro, North Carolina) was unable to visit some of the congregations under his supervision because of distance, finances, and the lack of time.

64. See Memorial 409, 1956 *Proceedings*, 752-53.

65. See "What Synod Says . . . Synodical Resolutions 1975-1986 . . . About Multicultural Ministry," published by the Board for Parish Services, The Lutheran Church—Missouri Synod, n. d.

66. 1962 Resolution 2-20 "To Develop a Synodwide Mission Approach to the Negro American," 1962 *Proceedings*, 97; Overtures 9-05A-B, 1981 *Convention Workbook*, 313.

67. 1981 Resolution 9-01 "To Open Every Ministry to Black Professional Church Workers," 1981 *Proceedings*, 209.

68. 1981 Resolution 6-20A "To Consider Employment of Black Faculty and Professional Staff," 1981 *Proceedings*, 193.

69. See *A Preliminary Report of the Review of District College and Agency Data*, Summit Conference of Synodical Leaders Involved in Black Ministry, St. Louis, January 31st–February 2nd, 1985.

70. *Webster's New World Dictionary*, Second College Edition (1970), s.v. "Integration."

71. In 1967 the Lutheran Church in America took the position that integration is a goal of the white majority (1967 Consultation of the Coordinating Committee of the Lutheran Church in America). Leronne Bennett says forthrightly that when the terms "assimilation" and "integration" are used, "the standard reference is white, the orientation is white," that is, "integration means [the] interaction of blacks and whites within a context of white supremacy" (Chester L. Hunt and Lewis Walker, *Ethnic Dynamics* [Homewood, IL: The Dorsey Press, 1974], 354).

72. Personal memorandum from Dr. Jeff Johnson.

73. The concept of "race," first used at the end of the eighteenth century, was a new tool used by Europeans to organize their understanding of themselves and the entire human family. That theory (i.e., the existence of a number of distinctive biological categories) is the way Europeans sought to make sense of and "locate" themselves in a world that was suddenly made larger and populated with more diverse peoples. Race was their way of solving the identity crisis precipitated by the very rapid expansion of their world. See *Encyclopedia of Sociology*, 1992 edition, s.v. "Race."

74. This position has been advanced most thoroughly by the anthropologist Victor Turner. He believes that this is one explanation for the growth of the number of religious groups (some of which we might label as highly esoteric), as well as an increase in religious behavior in American society (Victor Witter Turner, *The Ritual Process: Structure and Anti-Structure* [Chicago: Aldine Publishing Co., 1969]).

75. Shelby Steele states, "I think one of the heaviest weights that oppression leaves on the shoulders of its former victims is simply the memory of itself. This memory is a weight because it pulls the oppression forward, out of history and into the present, so that the former victim may see this world as much through the memory of his oppression

as through his experience in the present" (*The Content of Our Character*, 150).

76. Ernst Käsemann, *Commentary on Romans*, trans. and ed. Geoffrey W. Bromiley (Grand Rapids: Wm. B. Eerdmans, 1980), 49.

77. LC I, 3.

78. Matthew's genealogy not only traces Jesus' descent from Abraham, placing him in the mainstream of Israel's history, but also makes it clear that his was a "mixed bloodline." His ancestors include (1) Thamar or Tamar (a Canaanite, a non-Israelite who engaged in prostitution and bore Perez, and an ancestor of David); (2) Rachab or Rahab (also a Canaanite, a non-Israelite, a prostitute, the mother of Boaz, Ruth's husband); (3) Ruth (a Moabitess, a non-Israelite, descended from Lot's incest with his daughters, and the grandmother of David); and (4) Bathsheba (a Hittite, a non-Israelite, who bore David's progeny). According to the tenets of racist ideology, Jesus was a mixed-race Savior (cf. Ray Bakke, *The Urban Christian* [Downers Grove, IL: InterVarsity Press, 1987], 75-76). Luke's genealogy traces Jesus all the way back to Adam, and through Adam to God. Its intent is to signal what the rest of Luke's gospel makes clear, viz., that Jesus is the Savior of all.

79. Alan Davies writes in this connection, "In itself, there is nothing wrong in the attempt of Christians with different national and racial origins to claim Christ as their own; indeed, unless the Christian saviour belongs in some sense to all Christians and all types of Christians, Christian universalism is devoid of real significance. It is legitimate, therefore, for national churches to portray Christ as German, Latin, Anglo-Saxon, Afrikaner, or black—not to mention a score of other possibilities—*provided* both that he is not confined exclusively to any of these national and racial classifications and that the Jesus of history—a Jew of the first century—is not obscured behind the Christ of faith, so that his initial and essential Jewishness is downgraded or abolished" (Davies, *Infected Christianity*, 117).

80. Rudolf Siebert, "The Phenomenon of Racism" in *The Church and Racism*, 4.

81. See Markus Barth, *Ephesians*, in *The Anchor Bible* series (New York: Doubleday and Company, Inc., 1974), 1:291.

82. In his classic work on Ephesians, John Mackay wrote that Ephesians *"presents the basic structure* which humanity needs for true expression of the communal life. That structure is the fellowship of believers in Jesus Christ, which constitutes the essence of what we call the Christian Church. The Church is the universal community designed by God to transcend and embrace all differences of race, station, and sex that divide mankind. It constitutes the pattern for all true community, so that the surest way to achieve human harmony in the secular order is to extend the bounds of the Christian community throughout the world. For it is the measure in which men are reconciled to God, practice the worship of God, seek the Kingdom of God, and live with one another in peace as Christian brethren, that society shall be influenced, directly and indirectly, to seek peace and concord" (*God's Order* [New York: The MacMillan Company, 1953], 22).

83. Cultural imperialism is the attempt to suggest that a particular cultural way of worshiping is the only correct, appropriate, or acceptable way of worshipping God. Luther proceeded differently. His insistence that the people have the Gospel and worship in their own cultural idiom (e.g., his translation of the Bible into German, his introduction of ethnic hymnology, etc.) were important ingredients of the reformation of the church. The Lutheran confessional writings speak to this issue with unmistakable clarity. The Apology of the Augsburg Confession states that when the Creed speaks of "the church catholic" it does so to make it clear that the church is "made up of men scattered throughout the world who agree on the Gospel and have the same Christ, the same Holy Spirit, and the same sacraments, whether they have the same human traditions or not" (Ap VII and VIII, 10). The church is properly defined to avoid the mistaken impression that it is "only the outward observance of certain devotions and rituals" (*gewisse Ordnung etlicher Cerimonien und Gottesdiensts*; 13).

"For the true unity of the church it is enough to agree concerning the teaching of the Gospel and the administration of the sacraments. It is not necessary that human traditions and rites and ceremonies, instituted by men, should be alike everywhere" (30). The unity of the church is not harmed by "differences in rites instituted by men" (33). The apostles themselves "adapted in modified form to the Gospel history" "certain Old Testament customs" (40). Even accommodation to mistaken traditions regarding the time of the celebration of Easter is permissible without burden of conscience (see citation from Epiphanius, 42).

84. Cultural racism raises an issue of particular importance to the church. When the Synodical Conference first began working with African Americans in 1877, it found that in every city it entered (e.g., Little Rock, Arkansas, and Atlanta, Georgia), by its own account, the majority of the black population claimed membership in a Christian church. In 1891 when the Missouri Synod was invited into what became its largest African American mission field (the Eastern Field), that invitation came from African American Lutherans (the Evangelical Lutheran Alpha Synod of Freedmen in America), that is, people who held the Christian faith. In 1916 when Rosa Young invited the Missouri Synod into what became its rapidly growing African American mission field (the Alabama Field), that invitation came from a highly committed Christian.

The history of this period reveals that our Missouri Synod fathers did not recognize fully that one of the more important integrating elements of African American life and culture is Christianity. From the beginning African Americans were labeled "heathens" and attempts were made not only to impart a theology, but to impose a particular cultural expression of Christianity on black converts as though the Synod possessed the only acceptable way of expressing the faith of Jesus Christ. One could not be genuinely Christian, as some in Missouri saw it, if one did not sing, for example, German chorales. The new converts were forbidden to sing spirituals simply because they were spirituals. The new African American Lutheran congregations had to be organized the same way German Lutheran congregations were organized. These were all imposed on African Americans when they came into the Lutheran Church on the grounds that they were important and necessary conditions of being Lutheran.

85. Andrew Greeley, quoted by Edwin G. Clausen and Jack Bermingham, in *Pluralism, Racism, and Public Policy—The Search for Equality* (Boston: G. K. Hall & Co., 1981), 228-29.

86. Paul G. Hiebert, in his book *Anthropological Insights for Missionaries* (Grand Rapids: Baker Book House, 1985), writes in this connection:

"On the cognitive level, the people must understand the truth of the gospel. On the emotional level, they must experience the awe and mystery of God. On the evaluative level, the gospel must challenge them to respond in faith" (54).

87. LC IV, 10.

88. The Lutheran Church—Missouri Synod historically has made a distinction between *communio in sacris* (fellowship in sacred things) and *cooperatio in externis* (cooperation in externals). The former relationship refers to fellowship with other Christians at the altar or in the preaching of the Word of God. The latter has to do with joint efforts in social action and welfare and in other areas not directly affecting Word and sacrament (See e.g., 1974 CTCR Report on *A Lutheran Stance toward Ecumenism*, 16, and 1967 *Theology of Fellowship*, 18).

89. As in the popular dictum, "If you gonna talk the talk then you gotta walk the walk."

CONTRIBUTORS

Vincent Bacote, Associate Professor of Theology and Director of the Center for Applied Christian Ethics, Wheaton College—Ph.D., M.Phil., Drew University; M.Div., Trinity Evangelical Divinity School; B.S. in Biology, The Citadel.

Anthony B. Bradley, Associate Professor of Theology and Ethics, The King's College—Ph.D., Westminster Theological Seminary; M.A. in Ethics and Society, Fordham University; M.Div., Covenant Theological Seminary; B.S. in Biological Sciences, Clemson University.

Carl F. Ellis Jr., Assistant Professor of Practical Theology, Redeemer Theological Seminary—D.Phil., Oxford Graduate School, Memphis; M.A.R., Westminster Theological Seminary; B.A., Hampton Institute.

Lance Lewis, Pastor, Christ Redemption Fellowship—M.Div., Chesapeake Theological Seminary; B.A., Temple University.

Juan Martínez, Associate Provost for Diversity and International Programs, Academic Director of the Center for the Study of Hispanic Church and Community, and Associate Professor of Hispanic Studies and Pastoral Leadership, Fuller Theological Seminary—Ph.D., Th.M., Fuller Theological Seminary; M.Div., Mennonite Brethren Biblical Seminary.

Orlando Rivera, Assistant Professor and Department Chair of Pastoral Ministries, Nyack College—Ph.D. in Organizational Leadership, Regent University; M.B.A., Rollins College; M.Div., Reformed Theological Seminary; B.A., State University of New York, Albany.

Harold Dean Trulear, Associate Professor of Applied Theology, Howard University School of Divinity—Ph.D., Drew University; B.A., Morehouse College.

Ralph C. Watkins, Associate Professor of Evangelism and Church Growth, Columbia Theological Seminary—Ph.D., The University of Pittsburgh; D.Min., Pittsburgh Theological Seminary; M.A., The University of Dubuque Theological Seminary; B.A., California State University, Sacramento.

Amos Yong, J. Rodman Williams Professor of Theology and Dean of the School of Divinity at Regent University—Ph.D., Boston University; M.A., Portland State University; M.A., Western Evangelical Seminary; B.A., Bethany College.

INDEX OF SUBJECTS AND NAMES

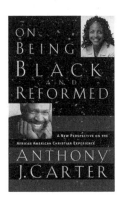

More Resources from P&R

Like the wounded man on the Jericho road, there are needy people in our path—the widow next door, the family strapped with medical bills, the homeless man outside our place of worship. God calls us to be ministers of mercy to people in need of shelter, assistance, medical care, or just friendship.

Timothy Keller demonstrates that caring for needy people is the job of every believer—not just church deacons—as fundamental to Christian living as evangelism, nurture, and worship. But Keller doesn't stop there. He shows *how* we can carry out this vital ministry as individuals, families, and churches.

Along the way, he deals perceptively with many thorny issues, such as the costs of meeting needs versus the limits of time and resources, giving material aid versus teaching responsibility, and meeting needs within the church versus those outside.

"*Ministries of Mercy* is a solid piece of work, the best of its kind that I have yet seen. It is concrete, down-to-earth, spelling out in specific detail every phase of what Keller calls the ministry of mercy."
    —**Vernon C. Grounds,** Chancellor, Denver Seminary, Littleton, Colorado

More Resources from P&R

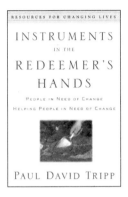

RESOURCES FOR CHANGING LIVES

INSTRUMENTS
IN THE
REDEEMER'S
HANDS

PEOPLE IN NEED OF CHANGE
HELPING PEOPLE IN NEED OF CHANGE

PAUL DAVID TRIPP

We might be relieved if God placed our sanctification only in the hands of trained professionals, but that is not his plan. Instead, through the ministry of every part of the body, the whole church will mature in Christ.

Paul David Tripp helps us discover where change is needed in our own lives and the lives of others. Following the example of Jesus, Tripp reveals how to get to know people, and how to lovingly speak truth to them.

"Helps us help others (and ourselves) by giving grace-centered hope that we can indeed change, and by showing us the biblical way to make change happen."
   —**Skip Ryan**

"A wonderful application of the old Gaelic saying, 'God strikes straight blows with crooked sticks.' As inadequate as we are, God is eager to use us to help others change. The more you apply the biblical principles discussed in this book, the more readily you will fit into his mighty hand."
   —**Ken Sande**